"*A Radiant Birth* is a true gift. Poetry and prose flow mingled dow
and soul. Lovingly assembled by two wise and care-filled wr
welcomes readers into the mystery and wonder of Advent. Thi
you will cherish and read year after year."

J. Brent Bill, author of *Holy Silence: The Gift of Quaker Spirituality* and *A
from the Heartland*

"Every legendary voice in this remarkable collection dares take u
brilliant star, the bleat of sheep, the crackle of straw, and evei
birthing to behold with anticipation and awe the remarkable
saving Jesus. In poems and memories told with astounding person
Chrysostom Society's communal exploration of the most holy
brave, amazing gift."

Patricia Raybon, author of the Annalee Spain Mystery series and *I Told t
Mountain to Move*

"Who better to lead us to the mystery of Word become flesh than v
better to help us sing songs of yearning and joy than poets? Thi
collection from some of my favorite writers and poets is a space f
nation to contemplate the incomprehensible gift of the incarnatioi
journey through Advent and Christmastide."

James K. A. Smith, editor in chief of *Image* journal

A Radiant

BIRTH

Advent Readings

for a *Bright Season*

Edited by Leslie Leyland Fields *and* Paul J. Willis

An imprint of InterVarsity Press
Downers Grove, Illinois

InterVarsity Press
P.O. Box 1400 | Downers Grove, IL 60515-1426
ivpress.com | email@ivpress.com

InterVarsity Press® is the publishing division of InterVarsity Christian Fellowship/USA®. For more information, visit intervarsity.org.

Scripture quotations, unless otherwise noted, are from The Message, copyright © 1993, 2002, 2018 by Eugene H. Peterson. Used by permission of NavPress. All rights reserved. Represented by Tyndale House Publishers.

While any stories in this book are true, some names and identifying information may have been changed to protect the privacy of individuals.

The publisher cannot verify the accuracy or functionality of website URLs used in this book beyond the date of publication.

Cover design: David Fassett
Cover images: Getty images: © Sarote Impheng / EyeEm, © Liyao Xie, © Baac3nes
Interior design: Daniel van Loon

ISBN 978-1-5140-0833-1 (print) | ISBN 978-1-5140-0834-8 (digital)

Printed in the United States of America ∞

Library of Congress Cataloging-in-Publication Data
A catalog record for this book is available from the Library of Congress.

30 29 28 27 26 25 24 23 | 12 11 10 9 8 7 6 5 4 3 2 1

TO THE MEMORY OF THOSE IN THIS BOOK

WHO HAVE GONE BEFORE US

St. John Chrysostom

Madeleine L'Engle

Eugene H. Peterson

Robert Siegel

Walter Wangerin Jr.

Contents

Part Two
Jesus, Born in Us

THIRD WEEK OF ADVENT

Part Three
Jesus in Us for the World

FIRST WEEK OF CHRISTMAS

SECOND WEEK OF CHRISTMAS

Foreword

RICHARD FOSTER

A Radiant Birth takes us between two glorious events in the Christian liturgical calendar: Advent and Epiphany. Advent is the four weeks before Christmas Day, guiding us into an expectant, hopeful anticipation of the miraculous birth of the Christ child. Epiphany comes at the end of the twelve days of Christmas, providing us with generous space for celebrating the wondrous revelation of God incarnate in Jesus, the Christ. Both events—Advent (the waiting) and Epiphany (the celebrating)— have one grand focus, which is to lead us into the ever-living reality of "God with us" in and through the person of Jesus. Indeed, the name Immanuel, in Hebrew meaning "God is with us," is the title given to the one and only Redeemer because it refers to God's everlasting intent for human life—namely, that we should be in every aspect a dwelling place of God.

We might call this reality "The Immanuel Principle." It simply and profoundly confesses that in and through Jesus Christ, God is always with us. It is a radiant with-God kind of life. Jesus lives among us as our Savior to forgive us, our Teacher to instruct us, our Lord to rule us, and our Friend to come alongside us.

One experience especially planted this reality deep into my heart and soul. I was approaching eight years old . . . young enough to be oblivious to the skeptic's arguments against the Incarnation and old enough to enter into the greatness and wonder of the

Christmas event. It was a Christmas Eve service led by Eugene and Jean Coffin, "my pastors," functioning so completely as one that I never separated their roles. Indeed, Eugene and Jean liked to refer to themselves as "a pair of jeans."

The Christmas Eve service itself was simple enough with Jean playing the organ and leading us in well-known Christmas carols. Then Eugene came forward, sat in a large rocking chair, and gathered us kids at his feet. He scooped up one small child and sat her on his lap.

In such settings children will often be nervous and fidgety. But not this night! This night a holy hush seemed to cover us all, children and adults alike. Eugene looked at us children, each one individually, lovingly, quietly. Then he opened his Bible and read us Luke's rendition of the Christmas story.

As I said, the elements of the service were quite ordinary. No dimming lights. No flickering candles. None of the things that are supposed to create just the right mood. It wasn't the outward, physical things at all. It was the holy hush that fell on us. It was "the Presence in the midst." It was the breaking in of the Shekinah of God. It was the overwhelming, interior, experiential reality of the Immanuel Principle, God with us. Even today, many, many years later, I still vividly remember that silent night, that holy night.

A Radiant Birth contains poems, stories, and essays by twenty-six members of the Chrysostom Society, a small fellowship of writers that two other colleagues and I formed several decades ago now. Hence, I have personally known each of these writers, some of them for many years. While we come from many branches of the Christian family, each one has a deep commitment to Jesus Christ and a genuine passion for the craft of writing. May I speak for our entire fellowship in hoping that in our words you will discover life-giving tidings of great joy.

Introduction

LESLIE LEYLAND FIELDS

It's Christmas morning, not yet light. I am ten years old, creeping down the stairs, and I am full of hope. My siblings and I were told there will be no Christmas. Our mother told us. She always tells the truth. But I believe in more than truth. Once our father surprised us on Easter with speckled chocolate eggs in the backyard. And once we had a special Thanksgiving with pies and everything and people were happy. I read fairy tales, too, and I've read *The Secret Garden* and *The Wizard of Oz*, so I know for a fact that the world can crack open at just the right time with a grand gift.

I float down the pine staircase, as light as a cloud, buoyed by all the happy endings I believe in. Just before I see the living room, I catch my breath and pause—maybe I even pray. There is likely a god out there somewhere, and maybe he is the kind of God who visits living rooms on Christmas. Finally I dare to look. There— the old Persian carpet, the wooden cupboard, the painting of the girl on the wall. And a deep echoing silence. I blink, deflate, fold to sit on the stairs. It is the Monday-Tuesday-always-everyday room without a tree, without tinsel, without the scatter of presents we had last year. Last year I got a blue bathrobe and a doll. My mother was right. Christmas is over.

And it was. But the loss grew lighter year by year. Our holidays had always been muted, sparse. There were no family gatherings to miss. There was never any money for presents. One year when we were young, my mother had a quarter to spend on each of us six kids. And we were not church people. What was there to celebrate then—our poverty? My father without a job and no prospects? This would be better, then. And there were compensations. Two of those Decembers my mother and the six of us loaded our tents and sleeping bags into our old Country Squire station wagon and drove to Florida to camp for two weeks in the sun. Who needed presents when we came back with a tan?

More than this, the *Plain Truth* magazines on our tables, my dour grandparents who were devoted Jehovah's Witnesses, and my mother all informed us that Christmas was a pagan holiday. As were all of the religious holidays, we were told. This was a bonus contributing enough self-righteousness to carry me through the long, empty holidays each year. Not celebrating surely made me more spiritual.

When, as a teenager, I discovered that a Savior had been born even for me, everything changed—except Christmas. My homegrown asceticism wasn't easily dislodged. I could not reconcile the unending holiday muzak and gaudy consumerism with God's entrance into the world. Shouldn't we be fasting instead of feasting? Shouldn't we be holy instead of happy?

Then I married. Several decades, a husband, and six children later, I am the magic merry godmother of all things Advent: light the fireplace, cut down the tallest tree, hang every ornament, set the table with a dozen candles, invite the neighbors, write plays, host open houses, make cookies for the sick, send shoe boxes overseas, make presents with the kids, and do it all with ribbons, sprinkles, carols, a real Christmas goose, and homemade wrapping paper of course! Most of all, don't collapse until after New Year's and Epiphany. And above all, perform it all with a holy mien, a contagious cheer, and a gentle, quiet spirit inviting Christ anew into your weary heart.

And every year I fail. Every year, come December, I vow to do better and still end up hosting these same uninvited guests—exhaustion, guilt, inadequacy, perfectionism, anxiety, failure—who push through my doors and shadow my every move. Maybe my mother was right. Maybe we should just let the baubly hullabaloo pass by our doors entirely. How much simpler and maybe more spiritual the season would be!

Don't we all do this? We all bring our complicated family histories to the season, which we live out in the midst of a noisy culture hawking its own version of celebration, and some of us add to that cacophony our local church culture, with its own peculiarities and traditions. Are the holy days supposed to be this hard?

No. Let's make it easier. Paul Willis and I are here with twenty-four others, wise guides all who will help shepherd us through the mistletoe wickets of the season. Let us start right now by turning around and looking behind us for a moment. How did the ancients in the faith observe the Advent season? Consider the first Christmas sermon preserved and passed down through the centuries. It was preached in Antioch in AD 386 by St. John Chrysostom, a priest who later became the Bishop of Constantinople. Can you see him standing in a cathedral, the gathered sitting beneath him? How did he begin? "Behold a new and wondrous mystery!"

"Behold!" Were they missing it already so soon, the wonder that "He who is, is born"? The miracle that "He who is above, now for our redemption dwells here below"? With eloquence and beauty and likely a measure of thunder, St. John called his listeners to holy attention.

Are we listening? One thousand six hundred and thirty-seven years have passed since that first sermon. More than two millennia now since God split the night with angels and delivered a bloody mewling infant from the body of a teenager. We try not to forget. We've created an elaborate web of remembrance and celebration. We hope we're doing enough. We wonder if we remember wonder. As the years go by, we behold through dimming eyes.

This is why we're here. We are here in these pages to behold, together, anew. We are following our namesake. All of us in these pages belong or have belonged to the Chrysostom Society, an informal gathering of writers of faith. St. John spoke so eloquently, so passionately that he was named *Chrysostom*, meaning "golden-tongued." We do not claim such eloquence, but we do as he did: twenty-six of us here use our pens to call ourselves and others to attention one more time. To behold—again. To hear the good news—again. To know hope—again. We offer up these poems, short stories, essays, and meditations as a choir of voices singing the "tidings of great joy" again.

The daily readings take us from the first Sunday of Advent through to Epiphany on January 6, the Twelfth Day of Christmas, celebrating the kings' worship and recognition of Jesus as the Messiah King. There are readings, then, for forty-two days.

We'll enter Advent, from the Latin *adventus*, meaning "coming" or "arrival," through three avenues:

Part One: Jesus, Born in Bethlehem takes us to the astonishing events surrounding his birth. Enter slowly. Let the familiar become strange and wondrous again.

Part Two: Jesus, Born in Us illuminates the holy disruption caused by his entrance into our minds and hearts.

Part Three: Jesus in Us for the World reveals surprising ways and places Jesus shows up when we walk our faith out into the world.

St. John's sermon ends, "To Him, then, Who out of confusion has wrought a clear path, to Christ, to the Father, and to the Holy Spirit, we offer all praise, now and forever. Amen."

May our stories, essays, and poems in these pages create a clear path out of confusion to heart-filled praise, joy, and hope, now and forever. Amen.

Part One

Jesus, Born in Bethlehem

THIS FIRST PART OF OUR ANTHOLOGY, "Jesus, Born in Bethlehem," is much what you would expect—a celebration of the coming and arrival of Jesus Christ in the flesh. We begin, then, with a passage of Scripture from *The Message*, memorably paraphrased by one of the longtime members of the Chrysostom Society, Eugene H. Peterson. Of course, there is painful waiting involved, a sense of being almost but not quite there, for that is the nature of Advent. But for the most part, the mood is one of tiptoe happiness, the childlike anticipation of tearing open a ribboned package that Philip Yancey so clearly recalls. But this happiness, to be real, is also tinged with sorrow. Tania Runyan and Lauren Winner take pains to remind us of the bloody reality of Jesus' birth—and of the death he is born for. But it is a birth and death for us. And so we say, in the words of St. John Chrysostom, "Praise this holy feast."

Sunday, Day One

Elizabeth and Mary Sing

LUKE 1:26-42

In the sixth month of Elizabeth's pregnancy, God sent the angel Gabriel to the Galilean village of Nazareth to a virgin engaged to be married to a man descended from David. His name was Joseph, and the virgin's name, Mary. Upon entering, Gabriel greeted her:

Good morning!
You're beautiful with God's beauty,
Beautiful inside and out!
God be with you.

She was thoroughly shaken, wondering what was behind a greeting like that. But the angel assured her, "Mary, you have nothing to fear. God has a surprise for you: You will become pregnant and give birth to a son and call his name Jesus.

He will be great,
    be called 'Son of the Highest.'
The Lord God will give him
    the throne of his father David;
He will rule Jacob's house forever—
    no end, ever, to his kingdom."

Mary said to the angel, "But how? I've never slept with a man."
The angel answered,
The Holy Spirit will come upon you,
　　the power of the Highest hover over you;
therefore, the child you bring to birth
　　will be called Holy, Son of God.
"And did you know that your cousin Elizabeth conceived a son, old as she is? Everyone called her barren, and here she is six months pregnant! Nothing, you see, is impossible with God."
And Mary said,
Yes, I see it all now:
　　I'm the Lord's maid, ready to serve.
Let it be with me
　　just as you say.
Then the angel left her.
Mary didn't waste a minute. She got up and traveled to a town in Judah in the hill country, straight to Zachariah's house, and greeted Elizabeth. When Elizabeth heard Mary's greeting, the baby in her womb leaped. She was filled with the Holy Spirit, and sang out exuberantly,
You're so blessed among women,
　　and the babe in your womb, also blessed!
And why am I so blessed that
　　the mother of my Lord visits me?
The moment the sound of your
　　greeting entered my ears,
the babe in my womb
　　skipped like a lamb for sheer joy.
Blessed woman, who believed what God said,
　　believed every word would come true!

Redeeming All Brokenness

MADELEINE L'ENGLE

As we move into Advent we are called to listen, something we seldom take time to do in this frenetic world of overactivity. But waiting for birth, waiting for death—these are listening times, when the normal distractions of life have lost their power to take us away from God's call to center in Christ.

During Advent we are traditionally called to contemplate death, judgment, hell, and heaven. To give birth to a baby is also a kind of death—death to the incredible intimacy of carrying a child, death to old ways of life and birth into new—and it is as strange for the parents as for the baby. Judgment: John of the Cross says that in the evening of life we shall be judged on love, not on our accomplishments; not on our successes and failures in the worldly sense, but solely on love.

Once again, as has happened during the past nearly two thousand years, predictions are being made of the time of this Second Coming, which, Jesus emphasized, "even the angels in heaven do not know." But we human creatures, who are "a little lower than the angels," too frequently try to set ourselves above them with our predictions and our arrogant assumption of knowledge, which God hid even from the angels. Advent is not a time to declare but to listen to whatever God may want to tell us through the singing of the stars, the quickening of a baby, the gallantry of a dying man.

Listen. Quietly. Humbly. Without arrogance.

In the first verse of "Jesu, Joy of Man's Desiring," we sing, "Word of God, our flesh that fashioned with the fire of life impassioned," and the marvelous mystery of incarnation shines. "Because in the mystery of the Word made flesh," goes one of my favorite propers, for it is indeed the mystery by which we live, give birth, watch death.

When the Second Person of the Trinity entered the virgin's womb and prepared to be born as a human baby (a particular baby, Jesus of Nazareth), his death was inevitable.

It is only after we have been enabled to say, "Be it unto me according to your Word," that we can accept the paradoxes of Christianity. Christ comes to live with us, bringing an incredible promise of God's love, but never are we promised that there will be no pain, no suffering, no death. Rather these very griefs are the road to love and eternal life.

In Advent we prepare for the coming of all love—that love which will redeem all the brokenness, wrongness, and hardnesses of heart that have afflicted us.

✳ Annunciation ✳

ROBERT SIEGEL

She didn't notice at first the air had changed.
She didn't, because she had no expectation
except the moment and what she was doing, absorbed
in it without the slightest reservation.

Things grew brighter, more distinct, themselves,
in a way beyond explaining. This was her home,
yet somehow things grew more homelike. Jars on the shelves
gleamed sharply: tomatoes, peaches, even the crumbs

on the table grew heavy with meaning and a sure repose
as if they were forever. When at last she saw
from the corner of her eye that gold fringe of his robe
she felt no fear, only a glad awe,

the Word already deep inside her as she replied
yes to that she'd chosen all her life.

Letter to Friends, Advent, 1990

JOHN LEAX

Twice snow has fallen
and stilled the chirring squirrel.
Its increase will end
the song Salvation Brook
sings trickling to the river.
But not yet.
The sun has life enough
to reach the trees.
Soon I will close myself
behind the cabin door
and spider my words
across the page
in propane warmth.
But not yet.
The fire between my shelter
and the chilling wind prevails.
What loneliness that drives
me out from you
to wait in emptiness as cold
slowly claims the land
will be assuaged.

But not yet.
The time of cold is not
the time to turn aside.
The dark will descend.
The wood will be held
in the lock of ice,
and the Word, quiet
as a star, will come.
But not yet.
These words are my words.
Wait. Wait.

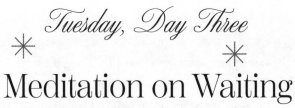

Tuesday, Day Three

Meditation on Waiting

MATTHEW DICKERSON

I delight in fishing. But fishing involves waiting. And waiting involves patience.

Unfortunately for the angler in me, lakes and even many rivers freeze over in the winter where I live. They turn from liquid to solid, at least on the surface. And this makes many types of fishing rather difficult. So November through January, the seasons of Advent and Christmas, usually mean only two types of fishing for me: fly fishing for steelhead and ice fishing for trout.

It's true that fly fishing is usually an active sport. I can sometimes traverse three or four miles of river in a morning of fly fishing. Even when I'm not migrating up or down a riverbank in search of a fish or a likely spot for one, I'm constantly on my feet, moving my arms. Nonetheless, despite all that movement, fly fishing still involves a lot of waiting. Days when my arm gets sore catching one fish after another are exceedingly rare. Far more common are the days when for every minute I spend with a fish on my line, I spend fifteen (or twenty or thirty or forty) minutes waiting for a fish to strike my fly.

Winter fly fishing for steelhead trout stretches patience even further. It isn't unusual for me to hook just two fish on a full day of steelhead fishing, and to land only one of them. I've had plenty of steelhead days without a single fish. A full day of waiting. I stand in ice water, making hundreds if not thousands of casts in almost the same place, drifting a heavy fly along the bottom of the river—where I can't even see it—waiting and hoping for a strike.

Indeed, the waiting begins even before I start fishing. The river where I most often fish for steelhead draws anglers from all across the region. If I want to get a good spot on the river, I have to beat the crowds. The legal fishing day starts half an hour before dawn. I show up an hour or more before that to stake out my claim. Then I just sit down on the cold wet riverbank and wait. In the dark and cold. With my thermos of hot coffee.

Then there's ice fishing, my other form of winter fishing. It may begin with a brief flurry of activity, but—even more than with steelhead fishing—it soon becomes an exercise in waiting. On the eighth day of Christmas, the traditional start of the ice fishing season in Maine, I head out onto the ice about an hour before dawn and drill five to ten holes through several inches of ice with a hand auger, all the while watching the eastern sky, waiting for the first hints of dawn. When the legal fishing day begins thirty minutes before dawn, I have the one flurry of activity as I rush to get all my rigs in the water: baiting each hook with a live shiner minnow, dropping them down to varying depths, placing my tip-up down in the hole I just drilled, and then setting the spring-loaded flags to alert me if a fish takes the bait.

Once all those tip-ups are placed, then I wait. I don't even hold them. I just wait. And wait. And wait some more.

Okay, some years I don't have to wait long. One year, the sun hadn't even risen, and I was just baiting my third tip-up when a four-and-a-half-pound landlocked salmon sprang the flag on the first tip-up. Dinner for the family appeared almost like manna from heaven. There have been occasional years when I've caught my limit of fresh trout by mid-morning. Most years, however, my flags are out all day just to bring in two or three fish. Some years, I don't see a flag up for hours. One year I didn't catch a single fish until the third day of the season.

As our climate has warmed over the past fifty years, the season for ice—and thus also the season for ice fishing—has noticeably shortened. On the lake in Maine where my family has spent lots of time, we wait longer each winter for the ice to form. Several years ago, we did two previously unheard-of things: we all dove into the unfrozen lake on Christmas morning for a quick "swim"; a year later we actually took the canoe out on New Year's Day. That year, I couldn't even ice fish until about the twelfth day of Christmas!

All that waiting recently had me thinking about Advent. In the Christian tradition, it's an important season that starts four Sundays before Christmas and ends on Christmas morning. The word *advent* comes to us from Latin, from a word meaning "arrival" or "coming." Despite the name, however, the season is not so much about arrival as it is about waiting. The arrival doesn't happen until the end of Advent. Christmas is the morning of arrival. Advent is the time of waiting for that arrival—perhaps patiently, or perhaps not so.

On the first Christmas roughly two millennia ago, the long-awaited arrival was a big deal. It was none other than the eternal God himself, the one who created the world, entering into his own creation in order to save it, taking on the form of a helpless infant baby born to a poor refugee family living in a captive nation. Jesus in the world. God in the world.

That period of waiting—the first Advent, we might call it—was a time of great suffering for many. The suffering had gone on for centuries, from when the prophets first foretold of a coming savior to the arrival of a baby in a manger.

On a really cold morning of ice fishing or winter steelhead fishing, I sometimes experience a small bit of suffering, which in the moment can feel like a great bit of suffering. I can do some preparation wearing my gloves, but at some point I need to take the gloves off and tie on a fly or grab live bait out of a bucket of ice water. I fumble around with cold fingers long enough to do the task, with an icy wind blowing needless pain into the exposed flesh of my fingers, down my spine, across my cheeks and into my eyes, making the task that much harder and slower. The truth is, though, that I choose this momentary agony myself.

And here is the real confession. Our cozy, heated family cottage with a pellet stove and a coffee pot sits right on the edge of the lake with windows looking out over the ice. That means that most of my ice-fishing mornings, once all my tip-ups are set on the frozen lake, I can head back inside for a cup of hot coffee. If I'm lucky, there's even a piece of leftover Christmas apple pie I can warm up in the microwave. And that's where I do my waiting: in a warm room with a hot drink, watching my tip-ups through the window. I only have to go outside if one of those orange flags actually pops up, and even then I only stay out long enough to pull in a fish and rebait my hook.

But two thousand years ago, those who were waiting for the long-promised Savior of the world had no choice about their suffering. And for most of them, their waiting was far more unpleasant than anything I've had to endure. I think especially of the suffering of Mary and Joseph, the chosen parents of the Savior, who had been driven out of their homes by an oppressive government and forced to live as a refugee family that couldn't find a home to take them in. After living for a time in another city in their own nation of Israel, they eventually fled all the way to Egypt to escape political persecution. What do I know of this?

There is, however, one way that my experience fishing is at least a bit like the waiting of Advent for a special arrival. Though waiting may require patience and even stillness, it is not passive. Rather, like many modern-day celebrations of Christmas, it is supposed to entail preparation. The Savior entered into the world to bring peace, and also justice for the oppressed, the poor, the stranger, and the refugee (which may be why he chose to be born to a family living in oppression). If we want to welcome that arrival, a good place to start our preparation is by practicing the same sort of peace, hospitality, and compassion. In these ways, as we are out in the world, we find Jesus—the very one we are waiting for—already present.

Angel at the Nativity

TANIA RUNYAN

Oh, God, I am heavy
with glory. My head thunders
from singing in the hills.

This night will come once.
Enough bright lights.
Enough shouting
at the shepherds in the fields.

Let me slip into the stable
and crouch among
the rooting swine.
Let me close my eyes
and feel the child's breath,
this wind that blows
through the mountains and stars,
lifting my weary wings.

Joseph at the Nativity

TANIA RUNYAN

Of any birth, I thought this
would be a clean one,
like pulling white linen
from a loom.

But when I return to the cave,
Mary throws her cloak
over the bloody straw and cries.
I know she wants me to leave.

There he lies, stomach rising
and falling, a shriveled pod
that does nothing but stare
at the edge of the feeding trough
with dark, unsteady eyes.

Is he God enough
to know that I am poor,
that we had no time
for a midwife, that swine
ate from his bed this morning?

If the angel was right, he knows.
He knows that Mary's swell
embarrassed me, that I was jealous
of her secret skyward smiles,
that now I want to run into these hills
and never come back.

Peace, peace, I've heard in my dreams.
This child will make you right.

But I can only stand here,
not a husband, not a father,
my hands hanging dumbly
at my sides. Do I touch him,
this child who is mine
and not mine? Do I enter
the kingdom of blood and stars?

✳

In a Mad Mad World, ✳ God Welcomes Our ✳ Merrymaking

PHILIP YANCEY

I've always had mixed feelings about Christmas. As I sifted through memories of the season while writing my memoir, *Where the Light Fell*, I better understood why.

In my elementary school, Christmas called for a major event in the auditorium, complete with a concert by the school band and chorus. For some reason I volunteered to represent the first grade by singing a solo rather than playing "Song of the Volga Boatmen" on the piano. I chose "O Little Town of Bethlehem," and my mother wrote out the words on a card in case I forgot them. Foolishly, I also volunteered for the role of Peter Cottontail in our class skit.

My mother fashioned a fine set of rabbit ears around coat hanger frames, fixed them on my head, and pinned a fluffy cotton tail to the seat of my pants. I had the good sense to remove the rabbit ears before attempting my solo but overlooked my cotton tail.

The upper classes laughed out loud as I walked to the microphone, which rattled me so much that I forgot the words to the Christmas carol. I was too ashamed to look at my notes, because then everyone would know I had forgotten them, so I hummed an entire verse, trying to make my mistake seem intentional. No one was fooled. My first public performance—and last solo—was a lesson in humility.

Flash forward seven years. Like most siblings, my older brother, Marshall, and I had an uneasy alliance. We argued, we competed, we sometimes snitched on each other. At Christmas we would agree in advance how much to spend on our gifts to one another, often buying exactly the same present just to make sure.

Mother would beam as we each opened, say, a fold-out box of LifeSavers candies, with both of us feigning surprise that we had thought of the same gift. This particular Christmas we had agreed to give each other a transistor radio, and Marshall double-crossed me: I gave him a radio while in return I got a cheap rubber baseball.

We stopped exchanging Christmas gifts after that year.

My real ambivalence about Christmas, however, traces back to an event I have no memory of. My memoir begins with a defining event in my life that occurred on December 15, a month after my first birthday. My father, just twenty-three years old, died of polio, guaranteeing our little family of three a life of hardship and poverty.

My maternal grandparents drove from Philadelphia to Atlanta for his funeral, held a few days after his death. They insisted on taking all three of us north for a few weeks' respite to give my mother time to grieve and contemplate her future.

Before we departed for Philadelphia, the Yancey grandparents hosted the out-of-town guests for an early Christmas dinner. The Yanceys had a pile of wrapped presents waiting under the tree, and long-faced adults, still dressed in their funeral clothes, sat around watching two young boys tear open packages and play with their new toys.

Christmas might have been my favorite holiday—except for the dark cloud that settled on Mother every December, the month my father died. She valiantly went through the motions of decorating a live tree and stringing up lights, but her heart never seemed in it. She would occasionally burst into tears for no apparent reason, and Marshall and I walked on eggshells.

Even as an adult, I find it hard to enter into the Christmas spirit. Do I really need the presents that family and friends kindly send my way, some of which will be stored on a closet shelf?

The glittery paper, the sealed plastic that cuts my hand, the cardboard boxes from Amazon—they end up in overflowing garbage and recycling containers. And is it appropriate to burn yet more fossil fuels in order to illuminate Christmas, especially in the midst of a pandemic that has killed five million people worldwide? My brother spent last Christmas in an overcrowded Covid-19 ward. How many will share that fate this year?

I feel like the curmudgeonly Ebenezer Scrooge from Charles Dickens' *A Christmas Carol*. Then I remember the scene of Bob Cratchit's family scrimping to splurge on a Christmas dinner of goose, potatoes, and pudding. Tiny Tim, the crippled son of Scrooge's underpaid clerk, offers a heartfelt blessing: "God bless us, every one!" Without help, Tim will likely die for want of treatment the family cannot afford, the Ghost of Christmas Present informs Scrooge. The vision of that deprived yet happy family pricks the conscience of the miserly Scrooge.

In his book of sermons titled *The Magnificent Defeat*, Frederick Buechner mentions two qualities of *childlikeness*. First, children have no fixed preconceptions of reality. If someone tells them that the mossy patch under the lilac bush is a magic place, or that opening a certain wardrobe will lead to Narnia, they'll surely test the theory.

Second, children know how to receive a gift without worrying about whether they deserve it or if it indebts them to the giver.

They simply receive it, joyfully tearing into the wrapping paper despite the solemn faces around them.

Somehow, even amid the secularized trappings that drown out the truth of Christmas, we have not lost a sense of celebration. On a dark night in Palestine, the sky itself burst into song, and shepherds ran to locate its origin. Before long, astrologers would endure a camel journey from Persia in order to present gifts fit for a king—only to find a baby.

That celebration, too, took place against a background of tragedy that left mothers crying for their slaughtered infants and Jesus' family fleeing as refugees.

Some three decades later, a woman poured very expensive perfume on Jesus' head (Mt 26). A "waste" declared Judas—the disciples' Scrooge—for she could have sold it and given the proceeds to the poor.

In what has become one of the most misinterpreted passages in the Bible, Jesus responded, "Why are you bothering this woman? She has done a beautiful thing to me. The poor you will always have with you, but you will not always have me. When she poured this perfume on my body, she did it to prepare me for burial" (vv. 10–12 NIV).

No one could accuse Jesus of insensitivity to the poor and marginalized. He spent his life among them, and this very event took place in the home of a social outcast, Simon the Leper. Yet Jesus acknowledged that when something extraordinary graces our benighted planet, it calls for celebration.

Maybe I had it right as a thirteen-month-old, grinning with delight while the adults around me grimaced in grief. "Truly I tell you, unless you change and become like little children, you will never enter the kingdom of heaven," said Jesus (Mt 18:3 NIV). He knew better than anyone that his brief sojourn would not solve the injustice, sickness, poverty, and violence of planet Earth.

It did, however, ignite a flame of hope that has never gone out. For those who believe, his birth, death, and resurrection are darkly glowing signs of what God plans for the entire cosmos.

I wonder what the shepherds and wise men thought when they found the object of their search. In the words that slipped my mind during my first-grade solo, "The hopes and fears of all the years are met in thee tonight." Really? Could this baby born to Jewish peasants possibly bear that burden?

It takes childlike faith to believe in a reality beyond the grim one we know so well, and to keep celebrating regardless. Sometimes a child's eye sees best.

Friday, Day Six

Christmas Child

PAUL WILLIS

When you were born, sycamore leaves
were brown and falling. They sifted
through the stable door and laid their hands
upon your cheek. Sunlight bent
through cracks in the wall and found
your lips. It was morning now.
Joseph slept, curled on the straw in a corner.

Your mother offered her breast
to you, the warm milk of humankind,
of kindness. You drank from the spongy
flesh as you could, a long way now
from vinegar, but closer, closer,
closer than the night before.

She cradles you, O Jesus Christ,
born in blood and born to bleed,
for this brief dawn a simple child, searching
the nipple, stirring among the whisper,
the touch, of sycamore.

O Simplicitas

MADELEINE L'ENGLE

An angel came to me
And I was unprepared
To be what God was using.
Mother I was to be.
A moment I despaired,
Thought briefly of refusing.
The angel knew I heard.
According to God's word
I bowed to this strange choosing.
A palace should have been
The birthplace of a king
(I had no way of knowing).
We went to Bethlehem;
It was so strange a thing.
The wind was cold, and blowing,
My cloak was old, and thin.
They turned us from the inn;
The town was overflowing.
God's Word, a child so small,
Who still must learn to speak,
Lay in humiliation.
Joseph stood, strong and tall.
The beasts were warm and meek

And moved with hesitation.
The Child born in a stall?
I understood it; all.
Kings came in adoration.
Perhaps it was absurd:
The stable set apart,
The sleepy cattle lowing;
And the incarnate Word
Resting against my heart.
My joy was overflowing.
The shepherds came, adored
The folly of the Lord,
Wiser than all men's knowing.

Saturday, Day Seven

Jesus' Bloody Birth

LAUREN F. WINNER

I don't have the nerve to stand up on Christmas Eve and preach about the choreography of childbirth, but I wish I did.

I wish I had the nerve to preach about Mary's increased estrogen production, a few days before birth (estrogen that will soften her cervix, and help her blood coagulate after delivery). I wish I had the nerve to preach about Mary's and Jesus' pituitary glands producing oxytocin, which in turn allows Mary's contractions to accelerate. I wish I had the nerve to preach that Mary and Jesus have to cooperate in birth, as all mothers and babies do—Jesus' own head stretches Mary's cervix, which in turn triggers her pituitary gland to release more oxytocin, which in turn stimulates contractions.

I wish I had the nerve to describe all that in my Christmas Eve homily, but I don't. It would seem somehow impolite to pester the people in my polite Episcopal church with a Yuletide description of Mary's cervix.

I'm not alone in sidestepping the bodily details of Jesus' birth. Over the centuries, many Christians who have pondered the Nativity have imagined Jesus' birth as swift and painless. In these reconstructions, Joseph gets Mary situated next to some barnyard animals, and then he leaves—in search of midwives, or sometimes a candle. When he returns, he finds that Mary has already given birth: no assistance was needed, because her labor was a snap. Mary, after all, is without sin, and pains in childbirth, the logic goes, are a mark of the fall—ergo, Mary would labor, one text tells us, "without a murmur or a lesion."

No murmurs or lesions, and presumably no danger either—no danger of Mary's bleeding out, no danger of either mother or baby dying in childbirth. Theologian colleagues tell me it is heretical to suggest that Jesus could have died in childbirth. I acknowledge that it is speculative—though no more so than Joseph's going out in search of candles—but it seems to me a fruitful speculation.

In coming to earth, Jesus enters, bodily, into vulnerability. That bodily vulnerability culminates in Jesus' being put to death by the state, but it is vulnerability that also shadows his birth. Put bluntly: lots of babies died in childbirth in antiquity, and lots of mothers too. Jesus could have died in Bethlehem; the cross and the manger could have become the same moment.

Something important is lost, I think, in evading the details of childbirth. We evade them because we are uncomfortable—but of all times of year, Christmas Eve is not the time to evade Jesus' humanity. If we do, we are ultimately evading Jesus, choosing a polite Docetism over bloody Jesus.

Jesus, of course, is bloody in many senses. Jesus is the God who becomes blood-filled. Jesus is the God who will shed blood for our salvation, and nourish the church eucharistically with his blood. And Jesus is bloody in the sense of the English curse word, which may come, dictionaries tell us, from the phrase "by our lady."

The lady is Mary, and the adjectival curse comes about by contraction.

Silent Night

JEANNE MURRAY WALKER

for Marjorie Maddox

The holly bush stands by the peeling door
she stumbled through last night, under the stare
of curious eyes. She didn't make it far

beyond the first stall, so she lay down there
to let her body have its way with her.
Rubbing her back, he braced himself against the door.

Maybe she wished that she could give it up—
the greeting of the angel on her stoop,
her *yes*, the thousand future paintings. She would swap

it all to stop this lava. Not to erupt
with God. To halt the bleeding of the Infinite
into that barn. Peaceful? Silent? It was abrupt,

loud, violent. She was blown apart. Body went
one way, she went another. Just to keep her blunt
place in the world, she sent her eyes hunting

the holly: that woman, sister, aunt, waiting
patiently outside to help. As God came ripping
through—a wild train—her eyes kept holding

that tree. She rests now. Wind is leaking
into the barn, the animals are sleeping.
Outside, the holy holly bough is breaking.

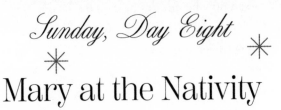

Sunday, Day Eight

Mary at the Nativity

TANIA RUNYAN

The angel said there would be no end
to his kingdom. So for three hundred days
I carried rivers and cedars and mountains.
Stars spilled in my belly when he turned.

Now I can't stop touching his hands,
the pink pebbles of his knuckles,
the soft wrinkle of flesh
between his forefinger and thumb.
I rub his fingernails as we drift
in and out of sleep. They are small
and smooth, like almond petals.
Forever, I will need nothing but these.

But all night, the visitors crowd
around us. I press his palms to my lips
in silence. They look down in anticipation,
as if they expect him
to spill coins from his hands
or raise a gold scepter
and turn swine into angels.

Isn't this wonder enough
that yesterday he was inside me,
and now he nuzzles next to my heart?
That he wraps his hand around
my finger and holds on?

Shepherd at the Nativity

TANIA RUNYAN

Last night I watched another wet lamb
slide into the dark and beheld this same
drowsy beauty: a mother bending toward
her nursing young. New limbs trembling.
Matching rhythms of breath.

The angels told us to praise and adore.
I spend my life trying not to love
such small things. But again and again
I carry my new lambs and name them,
play songs for them on the reed pipe,
bind their broken legs and search for them
in the foothills, until they are sold and worn,
served up, split open on an altar
and I feel my own blood rushing to the edge.

Monday, Day Nine

Winter Solstice

JAMES CALVIN SCHAAP

People I know have tipi rings on their South Dakota ranch, circles of stones visible only in summer, and then, only when cattle keep the grass down. But they're there, broad circles of half-submerged stones that mark the spots where, years ago, our indigenous ancestors pitched tents, footprints of a different time.

Those friends claim there's a long, straight line of stones in that pasture they believe points to the exact spot on the horizon where the sun rises on summer solstice. I haven't seen it, but I believe such things exist—ancient clocks to remind people that the times, they were a'changin'. Once the sun aligns with those rocks, people knew, regretfully, that winter was just over the hill.

Frederick Manfred, the Siouxland novelist, used to claim he knew where to find a similar straight line of rocks on Blue Mound, up the road in Minnesota. I never saw it, and you can't always trust a writer, but I'd like to believe it's there too.

Who knows? Maybe there are more. Out here on the edge of the plains, we still unpack our thick robes once we know winter is on its way.

The Lakota kept their history on buffalo hides. Maybe you've seen them. Somebody—the appointed artist, I suppose—kept track of calendar years by a single picture: a mule maybe, because that was the year some feisty donkey wandered into camp. The Lakota people call their sprawling history book hides "winter counts" because they once counted their years by the winters they endured. Winter counts. For the record, I have lived seventy winters. Now you know.

Out here, winter is the only season we can't wait to end the day it starts. No area chamber-of-commerce cheerleader tells tourists that people die here in sub-zero temperatures, but they can—and do. Thousands escape south, but most of us live with ice cube cars, frostbitten ears, and a drop of clear liquid on the ends of our noses. When it gets cold enough, you don't go out at all.

Long lines of solstice stones remind the people that it's soon to be winter. It's coming. Pull that buffalo robe up.

And then, right in the middle of all that miserable cold, comes Christmas. Right in the middle of all that wretched cold comes Hannukah, and right in the middle of all that hopeless cold hope itself rides up, the winter solstice, the flipside of the sun's annual pilgrimage.

In the Netherlands, Sinter Klaas arrives; in Germany, Poland, and the Czech Republic, St. Stephen. And Santa Lucia, candles in her hair and sweets in her open arms, comes to Sweden, Norway, and Denmark.

In the middle of all that cold comes all that grace, all that blessed warmth.

The angels on high appeared to low-life shepherds in the Judean hills at the very best possible time, a night of endless dark and awful cold, even in Israel. "Glory, glory," they sang, and the music couldn't have come at a better moment because those shepherds had to be sick to death of winter.

And thus Jesus comes to those who follow him, just when we need him most, in the cold nights of our winter counts.

Not everyone believes in the virgin birth, cattle speaking in tongues, or a king in a manger. Not all of us spend our nights lighting menorahs for a rededicated temple. Not many of us dance madly on winter solstice.

But out here where the wind blows out of some unseen northwest icebox, my goodness, do we need the joy of Christmas. We'd be groundhogs without the blessing of that first sweet "Noel."

Every winter, just when a frozen world seems hopeless, hope itself arrives to wipe that bead from your nose and mine: *Peace on Earth, goodwill toward men and women and children and all living things.*

Tuesday, Day Ten

Seeing a Great Light

You feed them from the abundance of your own house,
  letting them drink from your river of delights.
For you are the fountain of life,
  the light by which we see (Ps 36:8-10 NLT).

The land of Zebulun and Naphtali will be humbled, but there will be a time in the future when Galilee of the Gentiles, which lies along the road that runs between the Jordan and the sea, will be filled with glory.
  The people who walk in darkness
    will see a great light.
  For those who live in a land of deep darkness,
    a light will shine (Is 9:1-2 NLT).

"I will say to the prisoners, 'Come out in freedom,'
  and to those in darkness, 'Come into the light'" (Is 49:9 NLT).

Jesus spoke to the people once more and said, "I am the light of the world. If you follow me, you won't have to walk in darkness, because you will have the light that leads to life" (Jn 8:12 NLT).

For once you were full of darkness, but now you have light from the Lord. So live as people of light! (Eph 5:8 NLT)

I saw no temple in the city, for the Lord God Almighty and the Lamb are its temple. And the city has no need of sun or moon, for the glory of God illuminates the city, and the Lamb is its light. The nations will walk in its light, and the kings of the world will enter the city in all their glory (Rev 21:22-24 NLT).

Spreading Light in Our Wake

PAULA HUSTON

In the great scheme of things, light is actually quite rare. Geophysicists tell us that 71 percent of the earth's surface lies under the ocean, which means that most of our planet abides in eternal darkness. Astrophysicists add that over 95 percent of the total mass and energy content of the universe is "dark," which means that it is entirely invisible to us. Since our earliest beginnings, we have indeed been a people dwelling in a land of gloom and living under the shadow of death.

No wonder the predominant symbol in the Christmas story is light. The people who walk in great darkness now see a great light. The glory of the Lord shines down upon the shepherds. The great star of Bethlehem sheds its light over the manger where the child sleeps, illuminating the way west for the wise men and their camels. Epiphany, which commemorates their journey, is known in Greek as "The Day of Lights." Leo the Great says that for those who had no idea of what was about to happen, it must have been as though Jesus arrived "from a very remote and deep seclusion," spreading light in his wake.

Thanks to Christmas, we will never again be starved for light. This is why we celebrate Lucernarium during Easter Vigil, standing in the darkness as the priest lights the great Paschal candle, saying, "May the light of Christ rising in the glory dispel the darkness of our hearts and minds." This is why, on Christmas Eve, we stand and dip the candle in our hand into our neighbor's flame. One by one, we pass the light to each other until the whole room is afire.

Wednesday, Day Eleven

Somewhere in the Judean Hills: Part One

JAMES CALVIN SCHAAP

And there were, that night, shepherds in the fields, keeping watch over our flocks, when waterfalls of light flooded into the darkness, let loose by a legion of heavenly hosts.

It had been a night like any other, each of us keeping one sleepy eye peeled on the flocks while Ezra, the boss, ran through who would be camp tender or herders or lambers. When the angels appeared on the black stage, no one could look away. But the minute the angels left, no one could remember where they came from or how they'd appeared. Suddenly, a whoosh of silver wings. No boom, no charge, just a bath of sparkling brightness.

I thought I might have died and gone to heaven. When I shielded my eyes, I realized I had tumbled to the ground. There we all sat, sprawled out as if a mighty wind had swept through. The angels' firepower made the desert hills shine. *Stunning.* Even before those angels spoke, even before they sang—just *stunning.*

I cocked an elbow beneath me, and when the voices came, the words hummed like a lullaby line. "Don't be afraid," they said. The angels' words awakened a joy we'd never known that spread all over the Judean hills.

"Incredible news," the angels sang. "Not just for you guys but for all people." They said it again—"for *all* people. For everyone."

Their booming music erased every doubt. There we sat, bowled over, blind as bats in the astonishing radiance. "Today in the city of David a Savior has been born to you; he is the Messiah, the Lord."

Not one of us doubted. We should look for a sign, the angels said, a sign we couldn't help but chuckle about just a few minutes later as we picked up our things for the trip. "You will find a baby wrapped in swaddling clothes," the angels told us, "and lying in a manger."

"A savior—the Messiah!" Old Hadrian said, eyes starlight bright. "Honest to God, it's the Messiah!" He shook his hoary head. "In a barn?" He raised both hands. "Glory be," he said.

The hills turned inky dark again when those angels departed, but no one doubted what we'd seen because all of us had felt something pour like honey into our hearts. In ten minutes, no more, we were packed and ready to go to find this baby in "swaddling" clothes, whatever that was.

"Someone has to stay behind," brother Ezra said. "We can't all go. Someone has to stay with the sheep."

The moment he said it, I knew it would be the youngest—me. Couldn't be anyone else. The others were men. I was the kid. I'd be left behind.

"Surely the Lord will watch over the flock," Brom said, pulling his rucksack over his shoulder. "Surely the angels will keep an eye peeled." He pulled up his sleeves. "This is the Messiah—this is the King!"

"We can't just leave 'em alone," my brother said. "We can't take that chance."

"Bring them along," Brother Brom said. "Round 'em up and herd 'em to Bethlehem, the whole flock."

Ezra shook his head. "A roundup now? That child will be starting kindergarten by the time we get there."

"I'll stay," I said. "I'm the youngest. I don't want to—don't get me wrong." Ezra looked at me strangely. "But someone has to stay. Just make sure I hear the story when you return."

The silence made it clear I'd be the one.

"Bless you, Jesse," said Brom. "I don't know if it's right . . ."

"Just go," I told him. "Find the stable with the manger."

Brom mussed my hair. Hadrian punched my arm and squeezed my shoulder, and Arie laid his shepherd's crook over my shoulder and mumbled something about thanks. It was—and I knew it—one of the best things I'd ever done, but also the worst. The command had been clear: "Go to Bethlehem. See the miracle." Seriously, however, why wouldn't God's legions watch over the sheep on this very special night?

As soon as the men turned their backs, they were off, running toward this place called Bethlehem. In the pale moonlight, the sounds of their joy carried over open fields as if they were only an arm's length away.

I stared out into the deep, starry sky. Here and there, a lamb bleated, most bedded down in cloudy clumps in the moonlit darkness. *Lousy sheep*, I told myself. I'd become a shepherd because my father and my brother were, and so many others. I loved the sky and the long hills and stars all around, loved the end of the day—and the beginning too, the glorious light of dawn. But I told myself right then that I'd never really liked sheep all that much. They were needy and silly, and tonight I was stuck with them, alone in the desert hills with a thousand brainless sheep.

I looked for the highest spot on the land, then started to climb. Tonight, the night of the angels, my job was to watch sheep. I felt like bawling. I'd never been left alone with them before. Even though I knew volunteering was the right thing to do, my heart felt split as a melon because I so longed to be on the way to the King. There I was, alone, a million miles from joy.

The moon's glow opened up over the hills, and a scattered flock bedded down against stony ridges. I'd been around sheep my whole life, long enough to know their only sure defenses were noses that made them move into the wind, eyes sharp enough to pick out quick movements.

Maybe the choir of angels had worn them out, I thought. A million pinholes danced out of the nightfall. I turned east. The dawn was nowhere close to arriving. Ezra and the others wouldn't sleep— how could they? And I shouldn't. My job was to protect the sheep. I couldn't help but feel alone. I thought about a quick run back to get my baby brother, but Sammy was too little. I was alone and I was going to miss the biggest miracle of all—a king in a manger.

The sheep snored away the night. Nothing moved. Silence fell over me like a quilt, and my eyes grew heavy. I shook myself awake three times but heard no sound from the hushed hills. Painted images danced before me—a brand new baby wrapped in swaddling clothes, bathed in heavenly light, my friends all sweaty from the run, all of them on their knees.

"Glory to God in the highest"—it was like nothing I'd ever heard or seen before. I knew the night would be stuck in my memory forever.

I jumped awake. The hillside was so silent that my having to be there seemed silly. Who cared about sheep when the King had been born? I sat back, spread my legs out to lie down, and soon enough let myself go, bright ribbons of angel music playing through my soul.

"Jesse, the crook! Grab your crook."

I rubbed my eyes. A robed man was looking west, a white bandana around his head. It wasn't Ezra, Brom, or any of them, but I was foggy with sleep. Big shoulders, loud voice—someone who called me by name and knew I'd been napping. "Where?" I said. "What's happening?"

"Something's out there," the man said. "I can hear it—listen!"

A low rumble rose.

"Come with me!" The man pointed to my crook, then took off. I tried to stay with him, crook in my hand, sandals slapping over the sharp grass.

He put out a hand to signal me to stop. Still as a statue, he stood looking at a small flock rustled from sleep. He leaned into a crouch and signaled me to do the same. I was just an arm's reach behind him, and that's when I heard a hushed gurgling from behind a spiny oak cut in black silhouette against the night sky. A growl. A wolf. Probably two, maybe more.

A dozen sheep kept budging their way back toward us, snoots up against each other's flanks as they surged down the slope in reverse to keep the wolf in front of them.

"Behind the tree," the man whispered. "You take him, and I'll wait to see where the others show up." He pointed with his crook.

Ezra had taught me what to do when a wolf came, but I'd never stared one flat in the face, not alone anyway, until now.

"Go on," the man said. "That one may be the leader. If we run him off, the others may scatter—wherever they are."

The sheep kept staring at the shadowy oak while backing down the hill toward me.

"Just run?" I asked.

"You've got to scare him more than he scares you," the man said, nodding his head once more. "He's got to know he's not going to tangle with you."

The whole world seemed to disappear into the shadow created by that single oak tree. The low gurgling growl meandered toward them from somewhere out there, somewhere from behind the tree.

"Run! Go right at him!" the man said. "Just run."

So I did. I gathered courage into the tightest fist I could and took off, circled the flock to the left and ran directly at the tree, crook in my hand like a sword, until I came close enough to see him.

That wolf was even bigger than he'd been in my imagination, gray and dark and wide across the face. Bright and shiny eyes glowed with devil's glitter. I didn't move—not a muscle, as if I wasn't scared. I stopped a crook's length away so the two of us, frozen in time, stared wildly at each other.

"Scream!" the man in the bandana yelled. "Swing that thing in your hands and scream!"

I couldn't raise my arms. The monster wolf's eyes were glowing hot embers. His growl grew into something fierce, and he deepened his crouch as if to take a flying leap. I imagined myself being dragged to the ground, felt its teeth in my legs and shoulders.

"Run him off!" the man from town yelled from behind me. "Run him off!"

I took the crook in both hands and pulled it back behind my head. I swung that stick with so much force that I almost lost my footing. The crook thudded into the wolf's ribs, and that beast yelped like a puppy before scrambling off into the darkness.

"And don't you ever, ever come back, you devil!" I screamed.

When I turned around, I saw the sheep had vanished too, scared off just like the wolf had been. I wiped away my sweat with the back of my arm and looked into the darkness. "He was alone?" I asked the guy, without looking back.

There was no reply.

The sheep were gone, but so was he. I stepped back from around that spiny oak where the wolf had crouched, then listened, once again, to the sounds of nightfall, trying to hear any sound at all coming from the broad and hidden hillsides. No sound—nothing at all.

I had no idea where they'd gone—or the man in the bandana who had awakened me to all the danger. No idea.

I was alone in the darkest hour of night.

Thursday, Day Twelve

Somewhere in the Judean Hills: Part Two

JAMES CALVIN SCHAAP

I wished the others had seen the way I'd taken care of that ratty wolf, but then again, maybe they wouldn't care after following the angels into town for the baby King in swaddling clothes. Those fierce yellow eyes had made me nearly forget where they all were.

If it hadn't been for the stranger, there would be a very sad story to tell, for no matter whether that wolf was alone or in a pack, he would have feasted on a lamb or two, maybe ten. He would have then left them bloody and dead, or maybe still dying, while I slept. My brothers would return to find dead, mangled sheep, which would be terrible because the men would be so full of joy. That baby in swaddling clothes was the Messiah, the angels had said. Real live angels, too. Right in front of us, filling the sky.

Hours had passed now, and with every minute it seemed harder to believe that what the angels had proclaimed could be true. I looked up at the sky, at the darkness. I hadn't forgotten. How could anyone ever forget?

But who was the man who had appeared out of nowhere? Thanks be to God, I'd run off that wolf and done the job I'd been left behind to do. There would be that to say when the others returned.

I looked out into the darkness, then listened for stirring. No sound. I wished the guy in the white bandana would show up again because I needed to thank him for so much.

Stones rattled beneath the hooves of some pokey animal coming up the path, but when a snorting blast leaped out of the darkness, I knew it had to be Boaz, the old ram who always kept his distance from the flock—Boaz, the field general, who had a thing about me.

"Not to worry, sir," I said. "That wolf is long gone. Ought to be quiet now, I'm sure, even after all that music."

I dug my fingers into the wool behind the old guy's ears, just like I always had after he took me on. "You see 'em, Boaz?" I asked the old guy. "Did you see all those angels up there in the sky?"

Boaz nodded his hoary old head, then pulled away.

I got to my feet and stood for a moment. *A King in a manger*, I thought again. "You ever hear of such a thing, Boaz? How nuts is that anyway—a king in a barn?"

Boaz snorted then turned his head back and gave me a blank stare.

"Ah, you're a sheep," I told him. "I just wish I was there, you know—who wouldn't want to be?"

Boaz stomped off, looked back at me, snorted a couple of times again, and went halfway into the darkness.

Somehow, I got to thinking that Boaz maybe had something on his mind. I caught myself yawning again. I could feel sleep creeping back into me, but Boaz seemed to want to tell me something. I looked around, hoping to find the guy in the bandana, and I wondered how long it might be before the guys returned to tell me what great things they'd seen.

Then Boaz turned on a dime and charged me, came right up the path as if he wanted to knock me off my feet. Then he turned around again and trotted off into the darkness, lifted his big head, and bleated.

"Okay, okay," I said.

Just down the hill he went, toward some rocks, but he was always in the moonlight. I stepped along carefully through the sharp grass and stones, wishing I were as nimble as Boaz, whose shoulders rocked as he walked.

The ewe lay on her side, almost motionless, in a dusty circle where she'd tried to create a bed. When I came up beside her, I knelt down and put my hands on her stomach to be sure she was breathing. She had just now had a lamb, or maybe even two. I looked around to find them but found only one, in a puddle of afterbirth, dead.

The ewe's ribcage moved with a few faint breaths. She was still alive. I'd seen dozens and dozens of births, but I'd never seen a ewe quite like this. There was no bleeding. The lamb had probably been born dead, but it didn't look as if its mother had suffered greatly, even though it seemed she was dying.

"What must I do?" I said to Boaz, but the old ram simply stared. "I don't know what to do," I said. "She doesn't seem to be in trouble—it's almost as if she wants to die. Is that it? What must I do? Good Lord," I said, "I don't know what to do."

I got down on my hands and knees beside her and rubbed her head. I laid my arm around her and felt slight heaves through her body when she grasped for breath. She wasn't fighting. It was almost as if she didn't want to breathe.

I slipped my feet from under me so that my body would be closer to hers.

"You're doing it right," a voice said, a voice I knew belonged to the man with the white bandana. "Don't get up. Just stay right there—you're doing the right thing."

"Her baby is dead." I said. "I don't know what to do."

"Let me take care of that," he said.

"Must have died when she was being born, but there's nothing here that makes it look as if it was an awful delivery—not even much blood."

"You're doing the right thing," he told me. "Stay there. What that mother needs is you beside her."

"What can I do?" I said.

"Bring her peace."

"I don't want her to die," I told him. "I want her to live."

"You're doing the right thing," the man said. "Let me take care of things, you hear? You stay with her, just stay put—all night even."

"Seriously?" I asked.

"Every living thing needs comfort—every living thing needs love," he said. "I'll get her little one out of here. That'll help." He heard the man get back to his feet. "Just stay right there until morning—whether she lives or dies, she needs you."

When I felt her ribs, it seemed they were barely moving.

I didn't hear my brother and the rest of the guys return that morning, even though they were singing as they came up the side of the hill. I was sleeping. Big brother Ezra was in no mood to scold me for falling asleep.

"I'm so sorry," Ezra said, looming over me almost mournfully. "I was out of my head last night after the angels came." He slapped his forehead. "I should *not* have let you stay with the sheep—that was *my* job. I should have let you go."

"To the King?" I said quickly.

"The same. We found him all right, in swaddling clothes and lying in a manger."

"You were there?"

"In a manger and yet a king." Ezra shook his head.

"Praise God," I said.

Ezra's face was bright red in the morning light, as if he'd been looking into the sun all night long. "The angels were there—this time in silence, like all of us, even his mother. Just a girl she was, Jesse. Not much older than you. The King is the child of a child."

"And you were there?"

Brother Ezra took a deep breath. "I should never have let you stay. You're too young." His dusty robe danced beneath his long hair when he shrugged his shoulders. "I wanted so badly to be there at the birth of our King." He threw his arms around me. "You go now, by yourself, back to Bethlehem, go see for yourself," Ezra said. "My little brother needs to see the King."

My heart was hammering so hard I thought it might jump right out of my chest.

Still, there was so much to tell Ezra—the wolf, the stranger, the ewe who probably died. That's when I looked around. The sad mom was no longer beside me. Maybe it was all a dream. *No, it really did happen,* I told myself.

"How'd you get way over here anyway?" Ezra said.

"There was a ewe here," I said, but I realized it would be a long story, too long. "A baby lamb died, Ezra—and the mother . . ." He looked around. There was no trace of anything anywhere near. "I was with the mother," I said. "I was lying here with the mother because the man—"

There was so much to say, but no stories seemed so important as the Bethlehem king. Here, I pointed, because the baby, the little lamb, was already gone. The dusty earth around me was thick with tufts of sharp desert grasses, but no mother or baby.

"Never mind, never mind," Ezra said. "Go and see what has given all of us such joy." He reached into his rucksack and took out some jerky and berries and bent down. I felt my brother's kiss on the top of my head. "To us a child is born, to us a King."

✳ ✳ ✳

The hills seemed to fall away beneath me, little more than the smooth surface of the sea. I ran when I could, slowed to get my breath when I had to, climbed the hills like a goat, and streamed down the other side as if I were aboard a wave, the wind at my back. In my mind, I'd hidden away the map my brother had drawn in the sand, so I knew exactly where to go.

When I arrived, I slipped my arms out of my rucksack, wondering how one entered the palace, even if the palace was a stable. The doors were closed. Was I supposed to knock? Should I remove my sandals?

I licked my hand and pushed back the hair from my face, trying to look clean—not just some shepherd boy from the hills of Judea. There I stood at the door, listening for anything, even the cry of this baby, the King. Nothing. There was no sound at all.

Bethlehem was moving along as if nothing had happened—merchants opening their shops, mothers milling about and choosing what they needed, children playing behind me in the streets. Old men in gray beards sat on benches, leaning on their canes, pointing into the hills from which I'd come.

I knocked on the loose barn door politely, then pounded it with the heel of my hand. *Bang, bang, bang*—I couldn't have been mistaken.

I had seen the angels, too, and heard them; their voices were still ringing. "Be not afraid," they chanted over and over. I lifted the latch an inch or so, then waited, but no sound came from within. I wanted that glow I'd seen in my brother's face. I stood there, the door opened a bit, and a long shaft of light from the crack I'd made was running along the floor in front of me.

No one was there.

I opened the door wider, and light fell in all around. Just an empty manger in the center of the stable. A murky cloud of sadness pressed something inside me, tears from my own broken heart. No child who had become a mother. No angels. No king. No savior.

"He is not here, but he is not gone," a voice said, from the silhouetted figure at the door behind me. "Don't be afraid. He is safe. He is a child and a king, but he is not here."

"Where have they taken him?" I asked, running back toward the door. "My brother sent me here to see the baby King."

The man's face was guarded and dark. Then, in a flash that came to me just as those angels had done, I knew. The man in the bandana was back. He took a guarded look up and down the streets outside, then shut the door behind him.

"You were with me last night," I said. "You were beside me, all the time."

The man nodded. "I wish you could have seen him," the stranger told him. "But when King Herod heard of him, his parents thought it best to leave—they've gone to Egypt."

"To Egypt?" It seemed impossible.

"He is still the King," the man said. "Fear not."

"But I wanted to see him—I wanted to see the baby."

"There will be time," the man said.

"My brother said it was the best thing he'd ever seen."

"You will too," the stranger told him. "I know you will."

"Not here?"

"Not here, but in all his glory, he will return," the man in the bandana said. "You will see him yourself—I know you will."

"Not as a baby."

"Not as a baby, but never as anything less than King." He put a hand on my shoulder. "Now go back to the hills—go back to the sheep."

Honestly, I had to wipe back tears. "I don't want to go back—I want to see the King," I told him. "I want to serve the King."

"The sheep are his, my son," he said. "The sheep belong to the King. You will serve him as you serve them—as you did last night. They are his own." He bent down and looked into my eyes, his hand still on his shoulder. "Someday the King will tell the world that he is the good shepherd," the man said. "He will say it and you will know."

"And I will see him?" I asked.

"Face to face, I swear." And then he put his arms around me. "But it's time for you to go back to the hills, to the sheep. There will be a sign, too. It's time for you to be what the King wants you to be—like him, a good shepherd."

I couldn't help myself. "You're an angel, aren't you?" I asked. "You're one of those who came to us on the hills, out of the darkness—you're one of those who sang, one of those who told us to go to the city of David for Christ the Lord?"

Just like that, the man in the white bandana slipped away, disappearing into the half-darkness of an empty stable.

The hills never seemed so steep or so high as when I returned. It would be difficult to tell Ezra that no baby lay in the stable, that the King had been stolen away because King Herod wanted to find him.

The sun stood up above the hills like a great, golden shepherd, but the air was cool and light; and while the hike went slowly, I kept hearing the promises the angel in a white bandana had brought me.

When I saw old Boaz, the grandpa ram who had awakened me just last night, it was as if nothing had happened between us. The old guy gathered his gait into a run and came galloping down the side of the hill, his face up into the wind. He didn't stop for a moment but ran right into me, knocking me down the way he loved to do.

That's when I saw the ewe who had lost her lamb and wanted so badly to die. Right there with Boaz was the ewe I'd stayed to comfort, and she had made it. She was alive. There she stood beside Boaz.

"There will be a sign," that angel had told me. When I looked into the eyes of that mother ewe, I couldn't help but think she was the sign the angel promised, because it wasn't a dream—nothing that happened last night was a dream.

Then what he had told me was true too: someday I'd see the King myself. I'd hear him speak and say that he was the good shepherd.

Thanks be to God, I told myself. *Thanks be to God.*

The Prophecy of Simeon

LUKE 2:25-35 NLT

At that time there was a man in Jerusalem named Simeon. He was righteous and devout and was eagerly waiting for the Messiah to come and rescue Israel. The Holy Spirit was upon him and had revealed to him that he would not die until he had seen the Lord's Messiah. That day the Spirit led him to the Temple. So when Mary and Joseph came to present the baby Jesus to the Lord as the law required, Simeon was there. He took the child in his arms and praised God, saying,

"Sovereign Lord, now let your servant die in peace,
>   as you have promised.
I have seen your salvation,
>   which you have prepared for all people.
He is a light to reveal God to the nations,
>   and he is the glory of your people Israel!"

Jesus' parents were amazed at what was being said about him. Then Simeon blessed them, and he said to Mary, the baby's mother, "This child is destined to cause many in Israel to fall, and many others to rise. He has been sent as a sign from God, but many will oppose him. As a result, the deepest thoughts of many hearts will be revealed. And a sword will pierce your very soul."

Amo, Amas, Amat

PAUL WILLIS

In those student years that we lived in Spokane, Sharon and I eventually moved to a blonde-brick apartment house just west of downtown. Just across the hall from us lived an elderly couple from Plentywood, Montana. Henry Raaen was a Norwegian bachelor farmer until the age of forty-nine, when he married Minnie, a schoolteacher. She had played the organ at the Lutheran church where he had sung in the choir. They celebrated their fiftieth anniversary the summer before we met them. Mr. Raaen was now one hundred years old, and Mrs. Raaen was a spry eighty-seven.

One evening they invited us over for dessert, and by request I brought along my textbook for the Latin I was starting to learn. Mrs. Raaen had been a passionate teacher of Latin, and she often complained, or gloated rather, that young people these days were no longer interested in the Latin tongue. When I handed her my text, she found a line in the preface that she read to us with sad glee: "It is notorious that every year increasing numbers of students enter college without Latin."

She turned the pages slowly, looking up to tell us about a former teacher of her acquaintance who could not speak of the death of Julius Caesar without breaking into tears. "Sometimes," said Mrs. Raaen, "I lie awake at night reviewing my conjugations."

Then she got to the first set of verbs in the book. "Oh, yes," she said approvingly. Then, "Henry, do you remember the first conjugation?"

Up to this point, Henry had held a rigid silence. Part blind, part deaf, and chock full of arthritis, he nevertheless sat tall and erect in a bright red sweater and tie. The tops of his ears held deep, pale wrinkles. I wondered how his hundred-year-old mind worked.

He answered his wife like a cannon shot: "*Amo-amas-amat-amamus-amatis-amant!*"

Mrs. Raaen paged through the text for another five minutes, fondly absorbed. "Yes," she said, "I recognize most of the words on every page. But it would be too hard to get them all back. Too hard now to get them all back." Her face and voice were sadly resigned.

"May I make a motion," croaked Mr. Raaen, "that we put the Latin aside and proceed with dessert?"

Mrs. Raaen agreed, but then she happened upon the vocabulary index in the back, and the keyed exercises that go with every lesson. Dessert did not come for some time.

A few weeks later we invited the Raaens to our apartment to listen to *A Prairie Home Companion* on the radio. We thought they would be the perfect audience. For two hours they sat with us politely in our living room, the volume turned up very high, while Garrison Keillor said droll things about Lutherans and Norwegian bachelor farmers. Mr. and Mrs. Raaen gave the program their complete and stolid attention. They never laughed. They never smiled. When Garrison Keillor at last said, "Good night, everybody. Good night, now," Henry and Minnie rose to their feet with a kind of puzzled dignity and thanked us for having them. Then they left. *Exuent ambo.*

We later moved just upstairs from them, and from time to time we would hear a crash from below, indicating that Mr. Raaen had fallen off the toilet or out of bed. I would hurry downstairs and recollect Mr. Raaen into something like tranquility, and life would go on. Periodically an ambulance would come to the door, an occasion that Mrs. Raaen always met with sureness and solemnity. She would follow the stretcher out the door with head held high, arm in arm with the paramedic. *This was it*, she was thinking. After all these years, the final act, and she would march out like royalty. The fact that she got to repeat this performance several times in no way lessened the effect. She only improved with practice.

A few weeks before Mr. Raaen turned 103, just before Christmas, Sharon gave birth to our first child, a baby boy. Soon after we had brought him home, we took Jonathan down to the Raaens' apartment and into their bedroom, where Mr. Raaen lay cadaverously beneath the covers. With some effort he propped himself up and stretched out a hand of blessing upon the head of our little son. Consider then this giant man, well over six feet tall, with huge, spreading hands. Could Simeon in the Temple, when he met with the holy infant, have looked or acted any other way?

Then Mr. Raaen held out a five-dollar bill that he had hidden in the blankets. "From the oldest man in the building to the youngest!" he shouted.

That next year, of course, he died.

Nunc dimittis servum tuum Domine,
Secundum verbum tuum in pace.
Lord, now let your servant depart,
According to your word, in peace.

Saturday, Day Fourteen

Sermon on the Nativity

ST. JOHN CHRYSOSTOM

....

The first Christmas sermon preached and preserved.
Preached in AD 386 at Antioch.

B ehold a new and wondrous mystery.

My ears resound to the shepherd's song, piping no soft melody, but chanting full forth a heavenly hymn. The angels sing. The archangels blend their voice in harmony. The cherubim hymn their joyful praise. The seraphim exalt his glory. All join to praise this holy feast, beholding the Godhead here on earth, and man in heaven. He who is above, now for our redemption dwells here below; and he that was lowly is by divine mercy raised.

Bethlehem this day resembles heaven; hearing from the stars the singing of angelic voices; and in place of the sun, enfolds within itself on every side, the sun of justice. And ask not how: for where God wills, the order of nature yields. For he willed; he had the power; he descended; he redeemed; all things yielded in obedience to God. This day he who is, is born; and he who is, becomes what he was not. For when he was God, he became man; yet not departing from the Godhead that is his. Nor yet by any loss of divinity became he man, nor through increase became he God from man; but being the Word he became flesh, his nature, because of impassability, remaining unchanged.

And so the kings have come, and they have seen the heavenly King that has come upon the earth, not bringing with him angels, nor archangels, nor thrones, nor dominations, nor powers, nor principalities, but, treading a new and solitary path, he has come forth from a spotless womb.

Since this heavenly birth cannot be described, neither does his coming amongst us in these days permit of too curious scrutiny. Though I know that a virgin this day gave birth, and I believe that God was begotten before all time, yet the manner of this generation I have learned to venerate in silence, and I accept that this is not to be probed too curiously with wordy speech.

For with God we look not for the order of nature, but rest our faith in the power of him who works.

What shall I say to you; what shall I tell you? I behold a mother who has brought forth; I see a child come to this light by birth. The manner of his conception I cannot comprehend.

Nature here rested, while the will of God labored. O ineffable grace! The only begotten, who is before all ages, who cannot be touched or be perceived, who is simple, without body, has now put on my body, that is visible and liable to corruption. For what reason? That coming amongst us he may teach us, and teaching, lead us by the hand to the things that men cannot see. For since men believe that the eyes are more trustworthy than the ears, they doubt of that which they do not see, and so he has deigned to show himself in bodily presence, that he may remove all doubt.

Christ, finding the holy body and soul of the virgin, builds for himself a living temple, and as he had willed, formed there a man from the virgin; and, putting him on, this day came forth; unashamed of the lowliness of our nature.

For it was to him no lowering to put on what he himself had made. Let that handiwork be forever glorified, which became the cloak of its own creator. For as in the first creation of flesh, man could not be made before the clay had come into his hand, so neither could this corruptible body be glorified, until it had first become the garment of its maker.

What shall I say! And how shall I describe this birth to you? For this wonder fills me with astonishment. The ancient of days has become an infant. He who sits upon the sublime and heavenly throne, now lies in a manger. And he who cannot be touched, who is simple, without complexity, and incorporeal, now lies subject to the hands of men. He who has broken the bonds of sinners, is now bound by an infant's bands. But he has decreed that ignominy shall become honor, infamy be clothed with glory, and total humiliation the measure of his goodness.

For this he assumed my body, that I may become capable of his Word; taking my flesh, he gives me his spirit; and so he bestowing and I receiving, he prepares for me the treasure of life. He takes my flesh, to sanctify me; he gives me his Spirit that he may save me.

Come, then, let us observe the feast. Truly wondrous is the whole chronicle of the nativity. For this day the ancient slavery is ended, the devil confounded, the demons take to flight, the power of death is broken, paradise is unlocked, the curse is taken away, sin is removed from us, error driven out, truth has been brought back, the speech of kindliness diffused, and spreads on every side, a heavenly way of life has been implanted on the earth, angels communicate with men without fear, and men now hold speech with angels.

Why is this? Because God is now on earth, and man in heaven; on every side all things commingle. He became flesh. He did not become God. He was God. Wherefore he became flesh, so that he whom heaven did not contain, a manger would this day receive. He was placed in a manger, so that he, by whom all things are nourished, may receive an infant's food from his virgin mother. So, the father of all ages, as an infant at the breast, nestles in the virginal arms, that the magi may more easily see him. Since this day the magi too have come, and made a beginning of withstanding tyranny; and the heavens give glory, as the Lord is revealed by a star.

To him, then, who out of confusion has wrought a clear path, to Christ, to the Father, and to the Holy Spirit, we offer all praise, now and forever. Amen.

A Blessing for the New Baby

 **LUCI SHAW**

Lightly as a falling star, immense, may you
drop into the body of the pure young girl like a seed
into its furrow, entering your narrow home under the shadow
of Gabriel's feathers. May your flesh shape itself within her,
swelling her with shame and glory. May her belly grow
round as a small planet, a bowl of golden fruit.

When you suck in your first breath, and your loud cries
echo through the cave (Blessings on you, little howler!),
may Mary adorn you with tears and caresses like ribbons,
her face glowing, a moon among stars. At her breasts
may you drink the milk of mortality that transforms you,
even more, into one of your own creatures.

And now, as the night of the world folds you in
its brutal frost (the barnyard smell strong as sin),
and as Joseph, weary with unwelcome and relief, his hands
bloody from your birth, spreads his thin cloak
around you both, we doubly bless you, Baby,
as you are acquainted, for the first time, with our grief.

Part Two

Jesus,
Born in Us

THE SECOND PART OF OUR ANTHOLOGY, "Jesus, Born in Us," begins to answer the *So what?* question posed by the incarnation. As Luci Shaw reminds us, "Jesus himself gleams through / our high heart notes." Or as Diane Glancy confesses, "My wayward heart is the manger into which he was born." Or as Jill Peláez Baumgaertner testifies, "His spirit muscles us, he lunges / for our breath." Walter Wangerin Jr. tells the story of discovering the physical presence of Christ in his mother who has just taken Communion. "It's Jesus inside of me," she tells him. (That is a story he thinks might be from Easter week, but it might as well be Christmas!) In short, because Jesus was born, each one of us can be born again. And again. "Now," says the wise old man in Gina Ochsner's short story, "go and fly as only you can."

Sunday, Day Fifteen

Into the Darkest Hour

MADELEINE L'ENGLE

It was a time like this,
war and tumult of war,
a horror in the air.
Hungry yawned the abyss—
and yet there came the star
and the child most wonderfully there.

It was a time like this
of fear and lust for power,
license and greed and blight—
and yet the Prince of bliss
came into the darkest hour
in quiet and silent light.

And in a time like this
how celebrate his birth
when all things fall apart?
Ah! Wonderful it is:
with no room on the earth,
the stable is our heart.

Let the Stable Still Astonish

LESLIE LEYLAND FIELDS

Let the stable still astonish:
Straw-dirt floor, dull eyes,
Dusty flanks of donkeys, oxen;
Crumbling, crooked walls;
No bed to carry that pain,
And then, the child,
Rag-wrapped, laid to cry
In a trough.
Who would have chosen this?
Who would have said: "Yes,
Let the God of all the heavens and earth
Be born here, in this place?"
Who but the same God
Who stands in the darker, fouler rooms
Of our hearts and says, "Yes,
Let the God of Heaven and Earth
Be born here—
In this place."

Monday, Day Sixteen

No Silent Night

LESLIE LEYLAND FIELDS

O h Christmas! Last night I managed to string up one set of lights—the only holiday sparkle yet to hit my house. I'm sure one angel somewhere is clapping. I write this from bed, nursing a nasty cold caught on a long flight home last week.

When I got home, I found packages waiting. One from a dear friend who suddenly broke off our friendship and left town without explanation some dozen years ago. Now this Christmas gift with no note attached. I am confused all over again, missing her, hurt.

Throughout this holy month my email has been haunted by another sister in Christ. She heard a radio interview I did recently on forgiving my father and believes my view of forgiveness is "unbiblical." We are only to forgive those who express repentance first, she tells me. She feels God-appointed to correct my theology and is relentless in her pursuit of me. She is right to feel threatened. The unmeasured mercies of God are indeed unsettling, dangerous.

None of this has instilled much holiday spirit. We're all such a mess. Where is our "Silent Night"? Why aren't our hearts like the dear "little town of Bethlehem," quietly and plaintively waiting for a savior? Why are we fighting one another?

A few years ago, I went to Bethlehem just before Christmas and made a visit to the Church of the Nativity. Here I would find peace and good will. I would see the beauty of a people gathered from around the world to worship him.

But the church was in chaos. The enormous basilica was under renovation. Scaffolding crosshatched the interior, obscuring the astonishing pillars and ancient mosaic floors. Undeterred, people from all over the world stood patiently in line, filing past police stationed there to keep the peace. I, too, stood and watched and followed. All had come for this: to step down into the grotto, to kneel and lean into a tiny cavern where there was barely room for a single body. There, a silver star adorned the floor, marking the place where many people believe Mary gave birth to Jesus.

On this day, a tour guide stood just outside the grotto, pushing people through with piercing shouts of "That's enough! You go! Next! Next in line!" as men and women took their turn. Under the guide's watchful eye and ready tongue, each person hurriedly knelt to fit into the tiny space, flashed a photo of the star on the floor, rubbed an arm on its silvery surface, or swept a scarf across it while bodies pressed before and behind. One elderly woman in a headscarf lingered in her worship a few seconds too long. "That's enough! Too long! You get out!" the tour guide shot at her before impatiently waving in the next person.

After my six seconds on my knees beside the star, I emerged, stumbling, from the grotto. The air was abuzz with French, Polish, German, and Russian as groups marveled over the basilica, but then above it all, a shout came: "Stop! Stop talking! You!" I spotted a policeman in a distant corner, gesturing to the tour guides. The chorus of voices continued, unfazed. He tried again, louder this time, "A service is beginning. Stop now or I'll kick you all out!"

Above his voice and the tourists' mumbling, the drone of chanting began over in the Orthodox sanctuary.

What a mess! This church is occupied by police and six denominations that operate their own separate realms of this contested cathedral, all eager for a claim to the birthplace of Christ. Sometimes there is peace between them all—sometimes not. The police have broken up brawling priests on occasion.

The day wasn't over. Near the end, the guide unexpectedly took us to a glistening souvenir shop. It wasn't on our itinerary. He smiled and rubbed his hands and urged us all to shop till we dropped. "It's all on sale—a 20 percent discount, just for you!" he said with a wink. Two men approached us, ready to usher us to the cash register. Minutes later, we walked out, empty-handed, while the well-dressed owner came after us: "You must support us! You simply have to buy something here!"

It was not the happy day I imagined in Bethlehem. I found no peace on that small spot of earth. I found no silent moment, no light shining from dark streets—only shoving and shouting.

But maybe this is hopeful. Was Bethlehem so very different that day? Because of the census, everyone was returning to their hometowns, and the hotelkeepers were raking it in. The restaurants were overfilled. Every family rented out whatever room they had and charged too much. The noise, the dirt, the animal dung on sandals—everyone was busy making money and trying to get ahead. They paid no thought to a baby born in the hay that night. It was all an unholy mess.

Like me, right now. I'll never be as quiet or still as I want to be at Christmas. I won't make everything clean and beautiful. People will continue to send me strange packages and haranguing emails to which I will not always respond graciously. There will be dirty rooms and impatient shouts. There will be too many people at the wrong time and not enough at the right time. We'll try to profit from the season, selling our own wares—and we'll spend too much. My attempts to create a cathedral of worship for Jesus will likely be pathetic.

But Jesus already knows all of this, and in the end, everything will be all right. Because this is exactly the kind of place he chose to be born. This is exactly the kind of people he chose to be born among. These are exactly the kind of people he was born to save. And we are exactly the kind of people who need saving still. We don't have to clean it all up or perfect it first. We don't have to "fix" other people. We make room for the season in our own life and heart.

For unto you is born this day in the city of David, a Savior, who is Christ the Lord.

We kneel.

And enter in.

Tuesday, Day Seventeen

A Child Has Been Born—for Us!

ISAIAH 9:1-7

But there'll be no darkness for those who were in trouble. Earlier he did bring the lands of Zebulun and Naphtali into disrepute, but the time is coming when he'll make that whole area glorious—the road along the Sea, the country past the Jordan, international Galilee.

The people who walked in darkness
    have seen a great light.
For those who lived in a land of deep shadows—
    light! sunbursts of light!
You repopulated the nation,
    you expanded its joy.
Oh, they're so glad in your presence!
    Festival joy!
The joy of a great celebration,
    sharing rich gifts and warm greetings.
The abuse of oppressors and cruelty of tyrants—
    all their whips and clubs and curses—
Is gone, done away with, a deliverance
    as surprising and sudden as Gideon's old victory over Midian.

The boots of all those invading troops,
    along with their shirts soaked with innocent blood,
Will be piled in a heap and burned,
    a fire that will burn for days!
For a child has been born—for us!
    the gift of a son—for us!
He'll take over
    the running of the world.
His names will be: Amazing Counselor,
    Strong God,
Eternal Father,
    Prince of Wholeness.
His ruling authority will grow,
    and there'll be no limits to the wholeness he brings.
He'll rule from the historic David throne
    over that promised kingdom.
He'll put that kingdom on a firm footing
    and keep it going
With fair dealing and right living,
    beginning now and lasting always.
The zeal of GOD-of-the-Angel-Armies
    will do all this.

After the Annunciation

JILL PELÁEZ BAUMGAERTNER

He tumbles, toeing the walls of his captivity,
hears her muffled chatter, tastes the fog
of the sweet foods she eats, is startled
by the noise of saw on wood, the pounding
of nails. The amniotic fluid in his throat
teaches him to swallow. Much later, he
learns pain as his neurons begin
to fire. This was before.

After, he upends us as he somersaults
our vision. Our words, yes, he as Word
words us. We taste the savor
of the bread, the spice of wine,
his lifeblood coursing our hearts' chambers.
He is pulse born. He is pulse borne.

His spirit muscles us, he lunges
for our breath. He is where we are.
He feels the lilts of our delights,
the blazes of our sufferings.

Fresh as new skin, taut as nerve strings,
he drums and whistles us, our beat, our melody.
Our bodies know his gifts.
Our everlasting bodies.

Wednesday, Day Eighteen

He Came to Even Me: A Reader's Theater

  LESLIE LEYLAND FIELDS

CAST

Mary	Peter	Paul
Joseph	Herod	Julia
Shepherd Boy	Innkeeper	
Anna	Pilate	

NOTES

- The characters on stage are not frozen. They visibly listen and respond to those who come up and speak.
- In between the characters' entrances, congregational songs and carols may be added.

House lights are dimmed. Just soft lights on the platform.

Julia, in contemporary dress, slowly walks up the aisle to the platform, holding the Christ candle. She holds it almost reverentially. Places it slowly, gently in the center of the Communion table in center stage. She lights the candle. Stands for a moment regarding it, slowly walks back down the aisle.

Mary *walks down the aisle holding an unlit candle in a candlestick; she speaks reflectively.*

He came to me. . . . At the wrong time. I wasn't married—yet.
I was so young. I almost lost my husband because of him. . . .
I grew large and heavy, carrying him. He was heavy. He was
always heavy. Always weighed on my heart, especially as he
got older. I knew who the angel said he was. I raised him and
fed him and tucked him in at night, but I was watching him
all the time. Everything he did was so . . . so, right, so . . . good.
Even at the end. I knew he would make all things right. This
twisted, sorry world—he would make it right and whole
again. . . . I don't know why I was chosen. But I do know that
I was waiting for him. Maybe that's why he came to me—
because I was looking for him.

*She lights her candle with the Christ candle. Sets it down in front
of her.*

Joseph *coming from the pews or the aisle; holding unlit candle in his
hand; stands next to Mary; he looks at her, then speaks.*

He came to me too. First the angel came, and what he said,
I didn't believe. My betrothed is pregnant by someone else!
I was furious! This was not the Mary I knew! And then the
angel came and told me. I would have turned her out, her
and someone else's baby, if I didn't know. . . . Then he was
born. I hadn't been a father yet—what did I know about
being a father? But I learned, day by day. I loved him. Every
day of his life, I loved him. Mary and I, we never got over it,
that the God over all, YHWH, would choose us to raise his
son. No one chooses people like us . . .

*Joseph brings his candle, lights it from the Christ candle and sets
it beside her.*

Shepherd Boy *comes up from a pew; stands beside Mary.*

He came to me too. I was out doing my job, like I had been taught all my life. Taking care of the sheep. I watch them like they're my own family. I was kinda sleeping—we all were. It was night, the sheep were lying down, all asleep—and then it happened. The whole sky, like it burst, and like pieces of heaven falling out—all of these angels! It was about him . . . about him coming, being born and . . . I don't know why heaven opened up to us that night. Everything so white and bright and—holy! 'Cause we're the dirty men, they call us. We always stink like sheep, everyone says. No one comes around us. But he did! He came to us! Us dirty people . . .

Lights candle from the Christ candle. Mary and Joseph watch him do this.

Innkeeper *comes down aisle with a candle in his hand, but no candlestick.*

Yep, he came to me too. (Looks at the unlit candle in his hand.) I saw him, first in his mother's belly. I knew she would have him anytime—but my house was full! Every room in my boarding house—taken. I turned them away. I didn't have to. I could have moved some people around, juggled here and there. I could have made room in my house. But I didn't. I'd have to return some money. It would make my other customers unhappy. They didn't have any money anyway. So yeah, he came to me, and I sent him into the barn with the animals. I heard some of those shepherds calling him a king. . . . Kings aren't born in barns, you know? Not even in good hotels, like mine. King or not, I don't really care. But I'm not gonna just give my rooms away. It's a business. I'd do it again, too.

Looks at the candle in his hand, at their lit candles on the table, puts his down forcefully on the table. Walks to the side. Doesn't join the group.

Herod *walks up on stage boldly, swaggering.*

He *didn't* come to me. If he had, that would have made things so much easier! And you all wouldn't be standing there with your little candles. I heard about it: "A king is born. King of the Jews!" *I'm king!* There's no other king! Then came these astrologers, foreigners. They were going to find him for me! But they tricked me . . . they never came back. Well, there's more than one way to take care of the problem. I had them all killed, all the babies two and under. Simple. You eliminate the opposition. It's what a good king does. You think I did "wrong"? You want to blame someone? Blame those astrologers, those peculiar men. If they had come back and brought the child to me—I wouldn't have had to kill all the others. Just him! There's only one king.

Elbows everyone aside until he's right in front of all the candles. He blows out everyone's candle and tries to blow out the Christ candle—but cannot. Frustrated, he leaves to sit on a "throne" behind and to the side of center stage so he is still visible to the audience.

Anna *comes up, walks past Herod, gives him an angry look.*

He *was* the king; he *is* the king! He came to me too. But I had to wait a very long time. I was eighty-four. He was eight days old. Can you see that: me, the old woman holding this child, this just-born king? In the temple all those years. I told everyone the Messiah was coming! Not many believed me. Not many remembered to wait. Sometimes during those years, I think I forgot what I was waiting for. And when he came and Mary put him in my arms—*Mary, do you remember that?*—I knew it was true. All I had said, all I had hoped for: the Messiah! Come to save his people! And I just laughed, later, by myself.

That he would come to an old woman that no one cared about or listened to! I'll make the announcement again: the Messiah, the one and only King, has come to save his people!

She leads everyone in dipping her candle into the Christ candle to light it. Mary, Joseph, and the Shepherd Boy all immediately tip their candles into the flame with her so all are joined by the Christ candle. All remove their now-lit candles at once and place them in front of themselves. They all look visibly relieved, confident now.

Peter *enters thoughtfully, nods and makes eye contact with everyone holding the candles.*

He came to me out near the Jordan. My brother and I were following John the Baptizer. We thought he was the one! But he wasn't. It was the rabbi Jesus. Then Jesus asked us to follow after him. Well, I'm not sure if he asked or if he told us. I just knew I had to do it, to leave everything—my life, my fishing, working for my father. And he not only came to me—he *stayed* with me! He lived in my house in Capernaum! And that's what you have to understand. I'm a fisherman. Who chooses fishermen to turn over the world? Who chooses a man who's weak, who runs from danger, who betrays the one he loves the most? Who would choose that man to start his church? *His* church. He did. He chose *me*.

Ponders, amazed, lights his candle from the Christ candle. Sets it in front of him.

Pilate *walks regally down the aisle with a troubled, conflicted expression.*

He came to me—because I sent for him. I didn't know about his birth, but I heard all about him when he started doing those miracles. That's what everyone called them. Miracles. I wanted to see him all those years he was doing those . . . healings. Some claimed he brought a dead man back to life.

I called him to me because they wanted to execute him. The Jews did, his own people. They were dead set on it. It was my decision whether he lived or died. He wasn't anything like I expected. I asked him if he was a king, and he said, "My kingdom is not of this world." He *was* a king. I'm sure of that now. . . . I did it [*sadly, with regret*]. I turned him over to his own people [*defensively*]. I had no choice. If I didn't, there would have been a riot. I would have lost my job, maybe my head too. Yeah, he came to me, and I sent him to his death.

Puts his candle down on the table. Walks in front of everyone, slightly nudging them back. Blows out the Christ candle forcefully. Considers blowing out everyone else's candle but then decides against it. He picks up the unlit candle he placed on the table, goes to stand with Herod and the Innkeeper, uncomfortable . . . not feeling as though he belongs there, still holding the candle (down, not up).

Paul *enters walking briskly, with confidence and a sense of urgency.*

[*forcefully*] He didn't stay dead! Because he came to me too. I never saw him, like they did. But after he rose from the dead, he came to me in a blinding light that knocked me to the ground. I was killing his people. Yes, because I knew they would destroy our nation, our heritage. But I was the one destroying. Destroying the only light, the only truth. But it couldn't be destroyed. This is the power of Jesus Christ, to come to a murderer and give him a new heart, a new life. To choose a murderer to bring new life to others. And I would suffer too for all the suffering I caused. But there was no greater joy than this—to suffer for him. And for his church.

He came to me in a blinding light, and the light never died.

Everyone tips his/her candle into the Christ candle to relight it—and to light Paul's candle.

Julia *hurrying down the aisle.*

He came to me too. I can't believe I'm up here with all of you. You're all in the Scriptures! I'm just a normal person. I go to this church! It's like two thousand years later and he came to me too! I'm not sure why. You all were looking for him, waiting for him! Not me. I was over there. With them. Herod, you, Innkeeper. I get you completely! Who wants someone else to run your life, to be your king? I was queen of my own life! I did what I wanted. And it hasn't gone so well. I didn't rule my life. I couldn't even control myself. So, a savior is born. And he came to me too. He broke my heart. He took away all I thought was mine, and out of that, he made it all new. He brought living out of dying, took my darkness and made it light. And I know he did this not just for me, but for everyone!

She lights her candle from the Christ candle. Sets it down, then looks over at Pilate, the Innkeeper, and Herod. Herod and the Innkeeper look stonily back. Pilate is leaning, looking at her intensely. He looks between her and his candle, then looks longingly at everyone else, walks over to them, gently nudges Mary and Joseph aside, steps in, lights his candle from the Christ candle, and stands among them. Everyone watches him do this, accepts him willingly. All stand united, looking peaceful. Herod and the Innkeeper watch, unmoved.

Triumphantly

Mary: He comes to bring good news to the poor.

Pilate: The captives will be released,

Paul: the blind will be given their sight,

Joseph: the oppressed will be set free,

Anna: the old will be young again!

All: The time of the Lord's favor has come.

Men: And we call his name, Emmanuel, "God with us,"

Women: God who has come to us.

Shepherd: The dirty will be made clean!

Peter: The weak and afraid will be made strong!

Paul: The one with evil in his past will be forgiven.

Mary: The invisible ones will be seen and counted worthy.

Pilate: The uncertain will be given certainty.

Peter: The crooked will be made straight.

Julia: The selfish will love her neighbors.

Anna: The long-suffering will be rewarded.

All: For this day, in the city of David, a Savior has been born to you.

Joseph: And all those who confess the Lord Jesus with their lips
and believe in their heart that he was born to us,

Anna: and that God has raised him from the dead,

All: you will be saved.

Women: And every knee shall bow

Men: and every tongue confess

All: that Jesus Christ is Lord.

Julia: We bear witness to the truth:

Pilate: Light has come into the world—

All: and the darkness has not consumed it. The light of the world has come!

Everyone (except Herod and the Innkeeper) holds up their candles, following the lead of Julia.

Thursday, Day Nineteen

Star

EUGENE H. PETERSON

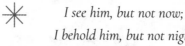

I see him, but not now;
I behold him, but not nigh:
a star shall come out of Jacob.

NUMBERS 24:17 RSV

No star is visible except at night,
Until the sun goes down, no accurate north.
Day's brightness hides what darkness shows to sight,
The hour I go to sleep the bear strides forth.

    I open my eyes to the cursed but requisite dark,
    The black sink that drains my cistern dry,
    And see, not nigh, not now, the heavenly mark
    Exploding in the quasar-messaged sky.

Out of the dark, behind my back, a sun
Launched light-years ago completes its run.

    The undeciphered skies of myth and story
    Now narrate the cadenced runes of glory.

Lost pilots wait for night to plot their flight,
Just so diurnal pilgrims praise the midnight.

Star Song

LUCI SHAW

We have been having
epiphanies like suns,
all this year long.
And now, at its close
when the planets
are shining through frost,
light runs
like music in the bones,
and the heart keeps rising
at the sound of any song.
An old magic flows
at the silver calling
of a bell,
rounding,
high and clear,
flying, falling,
sounding
the death knell
of our old year,
the new appearing
of Christ, our Morning Star.

Now, burst!
all our bell throats.
Toll!
every clapper tongue.
Stun the still night!
Jesus himself gleams through
our high heart notes
(it is no fable).
It is he whose light
glistens in each song sung
and in the true
coming together again
to the stable
of all of us: shepherds,
sages, his women and men,
common and faithful,
wealthy and wise,
with carillon hearts
and, suddenly,
stars in our eyes.

Friday, Day Twenty

✳ Orphan Christmas

DANIEL TAYLOR

✳ story that still bothers you sixty years after it happened
might be a story to pay attention to. I have more family
Christmas stories in my head than stories from any
other part of our shared life, but only one that seems unfinished.

There's the time when a bicycle fell out of the sky from Santa's
sleigh. Or so I thought. And the Christmas we three boys gave our
mother a basketball—and she pretended to love it. And the one where
my never-quite-successful father accepted the gift of a Christmas tree
lot on Christmas Eve morning, with the understanding that he was
responsible for getting rid of any trees he didn't sell. We boys sat with
him all day long, he drinking the eggnog my mother had sent him out
for, she wondering where we were. Total sales: one tree. Not enough
to cover the eggnog, much less getting rid of the trees.

But there's one Christmas story that still unsettles me, six decades after the fact. It was the year our youngest brother Mark
gave Steve and me an orphan. Now Mark had a history of ques-
tionable actions at Christmas, including replacing the dining
room table in the middle of the night with a gigantic tree, stomping
all over the roof shaking reindeer bells for the benefit of the little
grandkids, and giving puppies to people who didn't want puppies.
But this was the topper.

Steve and I were teenagers. Mark was maybe twelve. None of
us boys had ever given the others a present, so I was pleasantly

surprised when he handed Steve and me an envelope while we were opening gifts. *So,* I thought, *little brother understands that Christmas is about giving, not just getting.* I was impressed.

And then I wasn't.

We opened the present at the same time, and each of us discovered the same sweet, smiling boy's face staring up at us. A child's face. With an unpronounceable name. From a greatly distant place.

"What's this?" I asked.

"It's an orphan," Mark said, shyly proud.

"What are we supposed to do with an orphan?" asked Steve.

It wasn't the most graceful—or grace-filled—way to ask the question.

"We're going to support him," answered Mark, his shy, prideful look dissipating like water spilled on a sandy beach.

Steve and I both laughed. A sarcastic, teenage-boy, you've-got-to-be-kidding laugh. In fact that's exactly what I said.

"You've got to be kidding, Mark. You can't give us an orphan to support."

He was wounded to the core.

"It's not just you. I'm going to support him too."

More laughter. It was Steve's turn.

"No, no, no, Mark. That isn't how it works."

"What do you mean 'how it works?' Isn't Christmas about giving? Aren't we Christians? Aren't we supposed to give to others, not just grab stuff for ourselves?"

All good questions, but all, in our view, irrelevant. I tried to explain the real world to my little brother, who was now both angry and near tears.

"It's fine to not give us a present at all, Mark. And it's also fine not to give us a present and to spend the money instead on supporting an orphan, maybe in our name. But it is not fine to give us the responsibility of supporting an orphan with our own money and calling it a Christmas present. It's just not something you can do."

I thought I was being perfectly logical—as teenagers often assume themselves to be—but of course I was being perfectly obtuse. Mark was leading with his heart. He thought that should be enough. The world ought to reward that. And I was answering his heart call with casuistry.

That Christmas was ruined for Mark. It didn't matter what gifts he was given, the only thing he understood was that his own gift was rejected. We brothers put the orphan boy back in the envelope and never gave him another thought, confident that our analysis, and therefore our ethical standing, was unimpeachable.

I hesitate to draw a neat and lofty lesson from this story. But I can't help realizing, for the first time as I write this, that Christmas is all about an oft-rejected gift. God gave the gift, much of the world rejected it. Then and now, frequently on rationalistic grounds. Just as I rejected the orphan.

"That isn't how it works," we say about that gift—then and now.

We have become old men, Mark. I want to say I'm sorry. You were right. I didn't understand. We didn't understand.

Mahalia sang it better in "Sweet Little Jesus Boy" (Mark Hall, Bernhard Herms; Essential Music):

Sweet little Jesus boy
They made you be born in a manger . . .
Our eyes were blind, we could not see
We didn't know who you were.

And to that orphan boy you gifted to us—I hope someone else did our job. I hope you have had a good life, orphan boy, that you understood and valued the gift of it.

We didn't know who you were.

Saturday, Day Twenty-One

 Live Lightly

MARILYN McENTYRE

The ambiguity is entirely intentional. *Live lightly* in the sense of treading lightly on the earth and its vulnerable life systems. *Live lightly* in the sense of practicing a "lightness of being" that does not take oneself too seriously, does not weigh the spirit down with old resentments, forgives readily, and laughs because the comic dimension is redemptive. *Live lightly* by consenting and learning to be a "light bearer," inhabited and filled by the indwelling Spirit who gives us life.

Simply by being human we are light bearers. We emit energy. "Vibes" are a real thing. Some people (happily I know a number of them) bring light into any room they enter, subtly, unselfconsciously, probably also unconsciously. In their presence, hearts open and tense muscles relax. It is possible, of course, to hide one's light, not only "under a bushel" but deep within bodies and psyches that are injured, defended, and congested by anger, jealousy, or fear.

Living lightly is not possible, for any of us who have made it to adulthood, without some healing. Most of us need in some way to "lighten up." One thing that helps me do that when I find myself (or, these days, my country) in a place of darkness is to carry through the day a word or phrase or sentence from Scripture or poetry that redirects me toward the mystery of God's light—physical and metaphysical. I love, for instance, the phrase in the Nicene Creed that identifies Christ as "light from light." It brings with it an image of a lightfall cascading downward and outward, covering us with its plumes and mist. It is, for me, an image of abundance and exuberant, life-giving presence.

Or sometimes I find myself hearing and feeling healed by the simple assurance, "I am the light of the world" (John 8:12 NIV). Christ-light is personal—God with us and around us, immanent and intimate. Or the fact that gives us hope against hope in this bleak midwinter: "The light shines in the darkness, and the darkness has not overcome it" (John 1:5 NIV).

Living lightly is not only a spiritual practice but a way of going about daily tasks and entering into ordinary encounters. Sometimes a light touch is all it takes to exchange love or consolation. A light tap on the door can wake a sleeper gently who needs gentleness upon rising. A light once-over may be all it takes to make a house "fair," hospitable, and welcoming. And sometimes a whole morning is made more livable and productive by stopping to watch the sun rise "a ribbon at a time," or to wait at the window just long enough to see a hummingbird alight.

Freeman Creek Grove
Sequoia gigantea

PAUL WILLIS

Hiking down November snow,
we saw the first one still below us,
mounding up like a juniper
in the Shasta fir and the sugar pine.

Soon the trail entered its presence
(with Thanksgiving a day behind),
the trunk rising in dusky red, in fluted columns
strangely soft to our curious touch.

The first branches began at the tops
of other trees and continued into familiar wonder,
older perhaps than the Incarnation,
and longer rooted, and while they are here,
shedding for us new mercy of cones
flung green and small on the white of our steps.

We girdled the trunk with open arms,
unable to circumference it, much less
to find its center. In our random cries,
in the things we said to our wandering children,
I heard proclamation of peace on earth,
a wooden promise kept fresh for millennia,
the inaudible sound of a secret
seed in the South Sierra where eagles
nest in the falling snow.

Sunday, Day Twenty-Two

Maundy Thursday

WALTER WANGERIN JR.

How young I was at the period of my crisis, I do not remember. Young enough to crawl beneath the pews. Short enough to stand up on the seats of pews, when the congregation arose to sing hymns, and still be hidden. Old enough to hold womanhood in awe, but much too young to tease women. Old enough to want to see Jesus. Young enough to believe that the mortal eye *could* see Jesus.

I wanted to see Jesus. There was the core of my crisis. I mean, see him as eyewitnesses are able to see: his robe and the rope at his waist, his square, strong hands, the sandals on his feet, his tumble of wonderful hair, and the deep love in his eyes—for me!

For it seemed to me in those days that everyone else in my church must be seeing him on a regular basis, and that I alone was denied the sight of my Lord. They were a contented people, confident and unconcerned. I, on the other hand, felt like a little Cain among the Christians, from whom the dear Lord Jesus chose to hide particularly. No one seemed to tremble in the holy house of the Lord. But I . . .

Well, the knowledge of my peculiar exile came all in a rush one Sunday, when the preacher was preaching a mumblin' monotone of a sermon. One sentence leaped from his mouth and seized me: "We were eyewitnesses," he said. Eyewitnesses. We! I sat straight up and tuned my ear. This seemed, suddenly, the special ability of a special people to which the preacher belonged: to be eyewitnesses. Who's this we? What did they see? I glanced at my mother beside me, whose expression was not astonished. Evidently, eye-witnessing was familiar stuff to her. She was one of the "we." I took a fast survey of the faces behind me. Sleepy-eyed, dull-eyed, thoughtful-eyed; but no one's eyes were dazzled. None widened in wonder at what the preacher said. So then, they all belonged to the "we": eyewitnesses, every one of them! "We," the preacher was saying, "have seen the majesty of Jesus . . ."

No!

I didn't say that out loud. But I thought it very loud.

No, but I haven't! This was a stinging realization. *I haven't seen Jesus! My eyes were never witnesses!*

All at once the stained-glass picture of a praying Jesus wasn't enough for me. The Jesuses in my Sunday school books were merely pictures and a kind of mockery. I did not doubt that the Lord Jesus was actually there in his house somewhere—but where?

Even before the preacher was finished preaching, I dropped to the floor and peered through a forest of ankles, front and back and side to side—seeking Jesus perhaps on his hands and knees, a Jesus crawling away from me in a robe and a rope. But I saw nothing unusual and earned nothing for my effort except the disapproval of my mother, who hauled me up by my shoulder, but who probably wouldn't understand my panic since she was one of the "we."

For the rest of that service I sought in the faces around me some anxiety to match my anxious heart. But everyone sang the hymns with a mindless ease. I searched my memory for some dim moment when I might have caught a glimpse of Jesus. There was none. No, he'd never appeared to me. But he must be here, for hadn't he appeared to these others? Then why would he hide from me? Did he hate me? And where, in this temple of the Lord, would he be hiding?

Thus my crisis.

Sunday after Sunday I looked for Jesus. I ransacked the rooms of a very large church. I acquainted myself with kitchens and closets and boiler rooms—checking for half-eaten sandwiches, a vagrant sandal, signs of the skulking Lord.

One Sunday, exactly when the preacher stood chanting liturgy at the altar, I experienced a minor revelation. It seemed to me that the bold bass voice of the chant was not the preacher's at all, whose speaking voice was rather nasal and whining. It seemed that someone else was singing instead. For the preacher faced away from us, and the altar was as long as a man is tall, and the wooden altar (ah-ha!) was built in the shape of a monstrous coffin. Therefore, the real singer was lying inside the altar. And who else would that secret singer be—but Jesus?

I kept a shrewd eye on the altar for the rest of the service to be sure that he didn't escape. And after the service I took my heart in my hands and crept into the chancel, crept right up to the altar, certain that the Christ was still reclining therein, waiting in his tomb, as it were, till all the people departed.

Suddenly—*Ah-ha!*—I popped round to the back of the altar and peered inside its hollow cavity and saw . . . not Jesus. I saw a broken chair, a very old hymnal, and dust as thick as the centuries of human toil and misery.

For my restless soul there was no peace. I was not suffering a crisis of faith; never once did I doubt the truth or the presence of Jesus. Mine was a crisis of love—or perhaps of knowledge. Either the Lord had decided to avoid me particularly, or else I was stupid, the only one who did not know in which room the dear Lord Jesus abided. There must be one holier than all other rooms, one room so sacred and terrible that no one mentioned it, except in whispers and elders' meetings. Not the preacher's office. Dreadful as that room was, I'd already scouted it. Not the sacristy, nor the loft for the organ pipes, nor the choir room (which smelled of human sweat). A holiest of holies, a . . .

All at once I knew which room! My heart leaped into my throat with joy and fear at once. It was a room whose door I passed over with a tingling hush, whose mysterious interior I had never seen. Horrified by my own bravery, but desperate to see my Jesus, I determined to venture to the door of that room and to enter.

And so it came to pass that during a particular worship service during a very long sermon, I claimed the privilege of children and left my mother in the pew and crept downstairs all by myself to the forbidden room, the only room left where Jesus could be hiding: the women's rest room.

Oh, how hot my poor face burned at my own audacity at the danger I was daring. If the holiest place of the temple in old Jerusalem might kill an unworthy priest, how would this room of taboos receive a little boy? I swallowed and panted and sweat. But I wanted to see Jesus. I lifted my hand and I knocked.

"Jesus? Are you in there?"

No answer. None.

So I screwed my little courage together, sucked a breath, and pushed on the door, and it actually opened.

"Hello? Hello? Jesus—?"

I do not remember whether that was on a Maundy Thursday. It might well have been. It should have been.

With a deep, funereal gloom I returned to my mother. With a deathly sense of finality, I took the pew beside her. I was as woeful as any disciple who heard the Lord say, "I am leaving you, and where I go you cannot come." Abandoned!

Jesus does not abide in women's rest rooms. Mirrors are there, surrounded by lights and suffused by incense. But not Jesus.

Jesus was nowhere in this church for me.

I was a most sorrowful disciple. *Lord? Is it I? Did I somehow betray you that you would leave me alone in the night?*

With grim, remorseful eyes, I watched the service proceed. Perhaps my senses were intensified by sorrow, for I saw things as I had not seen them before. Things moved slowly, burdened by unusual weight and meaning. The preacher—far, far in the front of the church, robed in black and white—was lifting bread and mumbling. Then he was lifting an enormous cup and mumbling some more mysterious words I was likely never to understand: " . . . this cup is the New Testament in my blood . . ."

Blood. That seemed a grave word altogether.

"Do this," he was murmuring, "in remembrance of me."

Then people began to arise and to file forward. There was the deep timbre of song all around me. People were devout. Incomprehensible things were happening.

Then my mother got up. In marvelous docility, she walked forward down the aisle, away from me. My mother is a strong woman. She could haul me from the ground in one hand. This humility, then, was strange, and I stood up on the pew to watch her.

Far in the front of the church my mother diminished, almost to the size of a child. And then, to my astonishment, she did childish things: She kneeled down. She bowed her head. She let the preacher feed her! This was my mother, who knew how to make *me* eat! Like a little baby, she let the preacher lower the cup to her lips and give her a drink. Then she stood, they bowed to each other, and almost, as it were, upon a cushion of air my mother floated back to me.

Oh, this was a different woman. My mighty mother seemed infinitely soft.

And when she sat beside me and lowered her head to pray, I actually *smelled* the difference too. She had returned in a cloud of sweetness. I tasted this exquisite scent deep in my throat, and like a puppy found myself sniffing closer and closer to my mother's face—for the odor was arising from her nostrils, from her breathing, from within her.

Suddenly she looked up to see my face just inches from hers.

"What's the matter?" she whispered, and a whole bouquet of the odor overwhelmed me.

"Mama!" I breathed in wonder. "What's that?"

She wrinkled her forehead. "What's what?" she said.

"That," I said. I wanted to tug at her mouth. "That smell. What do I smell?"

"What I drank."

"But what is it? What's inside you?"

She began to flip for a hymn in the hymnal.

"Oh, Wally," she said casually, "that's Jesus. It's Jesus inside of me."

Jesus!

My mother then joined the congregation in singing a hymn with a hundred verses. But I kept standing on the pew beside her and grinning and grinning at her profile. *Jesus!* I put out my hand and rested it on my mother's shoulder. She glanced up, saw that my face was exploding with grins, gave me a pat and a smile, then went back to singing.

But *Jesus!* She told me where Jesus was at! Not far away from me at all. Closer to me than I ever thought possible. In my mama! He never had been hiding. I'd been looking wrong. My mighty mother was his holy temple all along.

So I shocked her by throwing my arms around her neck and hugging her with the gladness of any disciple who has seen the Lord alive again.

So she hauled my little self down to the pew beside her and commanded silliness to cease, but I didn't mind. A boy can grin as silently as the sky.

❋ ❋ ❋

And so it was that two commands of our Lord, delivered on Maundy Thursday, the night before he died, were twined into one for me. "Do this," he said of his Holy Supper, "in remembrance of me"—and in so doing his death and his presence would be proclaimed to all the world. My mother did it; she ate and drank, and as her faith received her Savior truly, she bore the Lord in my direction, and I met him in her.

And the second command was this: "Love one another." My mama did that too. And so there were two disciples side by side on the same pew. And one of them was grinning.

Old as Clouds, Wise as Wind

GINA OCHSNER

There once was an old man who lived on a small hill outside a village that held no fewer than 101 people on the weekdays and no more than 123 people on weekends, when relatives came to visit. Also living in the village were several dogs, three donkeys, and a multitude of cats, none of which will be included in the total count, although the man who lived on the tall hill just outside the village often felt the animals were more human than the humans. But that is another story for another time.

This man was as old as clouds and wise as wind. If he had a proper name, no one knew it. The people in the village called him the Bird Man. Though he lived alone in his small wooden house on the hill, he was never lonely. He had his workshop. And inside his workshop he had his birds. From pieces of aluminum, from bits of tin that the wind tore off rooftops and dropped on his doorstep, from the teeth of broken zippers, he made birds. Coils from the backsides of refrigerators and wire coat hangers became rib cages, breast bones, backbones. Curled metal copper shavings became eyebrows. Thin silver gum wrappers, layered one over the other, looked like feathers. Tiny ball bearings sprinkled along the feathers became freckles. He blunted small needles for feet and sharpened thimbles to make beaks. Each bird was built from whatever he had on hand, and no two birds looked exactly alike.

As he'd complete each bird, he'd lift it gently to his face and whisper. If someone were to look through the windows and watch him do this, they might think he was breathing into their beaks.

Now, there's all kinds of magic in this world. There's magic that can make things appear: like rabbits from a hat or gold coins from behind ears. There's magic that can change one thing into another so that a cascade of milk into a cupped hand becomes a shower of glitter when the hand is turned over and the fingers uncurl. But what the old man did was magic beyond magic. Because when he spoke to his birds, his voice swelled inside those little metal chests. The sound of his words made their wings rustle. His breath on their tiny bodies made their little hearts stir. Then with one, two, three flaps of their wings they lifted from his hand. In these magical moments his shop became a whirlwind of wings, a commotion of flight: joyous whirring and fluttering. And then, the old man would fling wide the door and out the birds went, curling into the sky like bright-colored scarves.

Because the people in the village knew that the old man made these birds out of old and rusted bits of metal—out of things they might have considered useless—they brought to him all their metal scrap. On a regular basis, usually on Tuesdays and sometimes Thursdays, villagers young and old ventured up the hill. Because he was as old as clouds and patient as soil, he never turned any of them away. He especially loved it when the children came, bringing with them their oily sardine tins, crumpled gum wrappers, and bent thumbtacks.

And whether young or old, his visitors often brought questions.

"What makes your birds fly?" they sometimes wondered. If it was a grown-up who asked, the old man would smile an apology. If a child asked, his eyes brightened, and he'd patiently explain: "I put a song inside each bird. Right here," the old man would tap the hollow insides of a tiny metal rib cage. "And then I tell the birds the words they need to hear, the right ones that will help them fly."

This answer satisfied most children, but every now and again one of them would demand to know precisely which words the man used. At this he'd shrug and smile. He was old as clouds, wise as wind, and he knew that not every good question must be answered. At least not right away.

He would not sell his birds, but sometimes he would give them away: one to each person who asked very nicely. "Take care of this bird, it is special, there is no other quite like it." Always people promised to do just that. But promises wear thin in time, and sometimes people would forget the gift of their birds. Sometimes they'd perch them in their trees, and the wind would carry them off. Sometimes people tired of their birds and put them in trash bins. Of course this made the old man very sad, and he'd go looking for those forgotten, neglected birds.

One child, a boy who was probably eleven or even twelve, became a regular visitor, trekking up the hill not only on Tuesdays and Thursdays but on all the days around and in between. He did not pester the old man with the usual questions. Day after day, week after week, he swept up the metal shavings from the wooden workshop floor and carefully blew the dust off them. He gathered the leftover metal scrap and washed the shop windows. The old man liked how the boy cleaned the work table, and he liked the great care the boy showed for the birds that the old man was making. Every day the old man complimented the boy on his hard work and reminded him: *You are much loved, boy. You are utterly unique, and there is no one quite like you.*

One day, after the old man had opened the shop door to set a new flock of birds free, the boy, who had in all these weeks and months become taller and older, turned to the old man. "Doesn't it make you sad when your birds fly away? Don't you worry where they might fly off to?"

Because the old man had been waiting for such a long time for someone to ask this question, the old man's heart swelled with joy. He knew that because the boy loved the birds, he could be the old man's apprentice.

"Follow me," the old man said, slinging a big burlap sack over his shoulder. Together they went walking into the woods. Sometimes the birds lost their way, the old man explained. Sometimes they grew tired of flight and fell to the ground where they became mired in mud or trampled underfoot. But because he knew each bird by name, knew everything about each bird, he knew where to find them. And he'd look and look for them until they were found.

The apprentice saw with his own eyes that this was true. The old man walked in those woods finding the lost or hurt or tired. When he did, he'd gingerly place them into his sack. That evening, as dark thickened around the apprentice and old man, they opened the sack and set the wayward, injured, tired birds on the workshop table. The apprentice figured the old man would pick up pliers and go right to work on the birds. But no. Just as before when the old man had first made each bird, he lifted them near his mouth and whispered something to it.

One day a stranger climbed the hill and peered for a long time through the workshop windows. Because the man was old as clouds and wise as wind, he could guess why the man was there and what he wanted. He was not surprised to hear the man tell him that he was a manufacturer from two towns away. "I will buy your design. I'll build a large factory, and you can be the supervisor." The man's eyes were like charcoal, and his voice was like soot.

"Some things are not meant to be bought or sold," the old man said, his voice heavy with sadness.

"But think of how many more birds we could make if we did it in a big factory," the visitor said.

"Each bird is peculiar, and individual. Every song they sing is completely unique. Even the way each one of them flaps its wings is different. This is why they cannot and should not be made in a factory in large number by large machines."

"But I could make you rich!" Now the man was flabbergasted. "You'd be famous!"

The old man did not need money. And he did not want to be famous. He just wanted to make his birds. And so, the old man gave a quick nod to the apprentice, who firmly shut the shop door.

For many weeks and months the old man and his apprentice bent wire and twisted metal. Together they put small sheets of it through the metal press, rolled it under heavy rollers to stretch the metal. Together they fastened wings to rib cages, feathers to wings. For many weeks and months, they worked together building and releasing birds that climbed the treetops, filling the air with their strange metallic songs.

It should be noted here that the apprentice loved the old man very much. He was like the grandfather the young man had never had. But he couldn't help noticing how poorly the old man lived: he had almost no food and very little heat, and he wore the same work clothes day after day. He couldn't help thinking that there might be a better way to make their birds, that maybe the factory owner's ideas weren't such bad ones. If they made more birds more quickly and sold them, they wouldn't have to wonder if people in the town below would remember to bring a little firewood and pieces of metal. They wouldn't have to give birds away for free and wonder if they were being well cared for.

One day the apprentice approached the old man. "I have been working with you for so long, that I haven't seen much of the world. I would like to go away for just a little while and see what the world outside the workshop and our village looks like."

"Of course you may go," the old man said. And the boy left. Days passed, then weeks. Then months. The old man began to worry. He decided to go looking for damaged birds in the woods. He put his big coat on and gathered his burlap sack. When he reached the wood, he saw beneath the trees something very strange. Small metallic birds littered the forest floor. The old man gathered them one by one, put them into his sack. They weren't the birds he had made, this much he knew for sure. For starters, not a single one of them had a bit of color. And none of them had wings that could actually move. It was clear that no one had breathed the words into them that they needed to hear.

Because the old man was old as clouds and wise as wind, he kept on walking through the forest. He knew when something was wounded and needed to be found. Sure enough, deep in the heart of the forest he found his young apprentice, slumped against a tree. How long the apprentice had been there, the old man couldn't tell for sure, but he could see that the young man was shivering with cold, and his face had grown long and thin.

"Why are you sitting there shivering with your face long and thin?" the old man asked his apprentice. "Why haven't you come back to the workshop?"

"I am too ashamed to come back," the apprentice said, and his voice was hollow like the chests of the broken metal birds.

The old man lifted the apprentice to his feet and put his own big coat over his shoulders. "Come back anyway." Now it should be noted that the old man, wise and patient, knew exactly where the apprentice had been and what he had done. But he also knew that sometimes it takes time for someone to find the right words to say what they need to. And so, they walked together through the woods, back to the workshop, carrying their silences between them.

When they reached the workshop, the old man pushed open the door and waited for the apprentice to cross the threshold.

"I can't come in," said the apprentice. "I'm not fit to work for you anymore. I sold your design to the factory manager so that I could bring you some money. But the birds we made were nothing like your birds. They could only fly for a short time in one direction. And then they'd crash and fall. All the money I made I had to give back to the customers."

The old man guided his apprentice to the long wooden work table. He placed a wire coil in the apprentice's left hand. "But why did they fall?" the old man asked, knowing full well the answer.

"Because I didn't know the right words to make them fly."

Now the old man placed a pair of pliers in the apprentice's right hand. "They are words you've heard every day while working in my shop." Now the old man leaned over the apprentice and put his mouth very close to the young man's ear: "*You are much loved. There is no one quite like you. Now go and fly as only you can.*"

Tuesday, Day Twenty-Four

Exile

DIANE GLANCY

Christmas was a time away from home. My father was transferred, and we would return to an aunt's house in Kansas City. When I was married, I lived other places and would leave to go to my mother's on Christmas Eve and my husband's mother's house on Christmas Day. It always was displacement.

Joseph and Mary also were displaced—traveling from Nazareth in Galilee to Bethlehem in Judea, the city of David. It was a decree from Caesar Augustus. All the world would be taxed and everyone went to his own city (Lk 2:3 KJV). "And so it was, that, while they were there, the days were accomplished that she should be delivered. And she brought forth her first-born son, and wrapped him in swaddling clothes, and laid him in a manger" (Lk 2:6-7 KJV).

I have recognized, over the long years, my wayward heart is the manger into which he was born.

And there was in the same country shepherds abiding in the field, keeping watch over their flock by night. And the angel of the Lord came upon them, and the glory of the Lord shone round about them: and they were sore afraid. And the angel said unto them, Fear not: for I bring you tidings of great joy, which shall be to all people. For unto you is born this day in

the city of David a Savior, which is Christ the Lord. . . . And
suddenly there was with the angel a multitude of the heavenly
host praising God, and saying, Glory to God in the highest, and
on earth peace, good will toward men. (Lk 2:8-11, 13-14 KJV)

I have heard the heavenly choir. Often we attended church ser-
vices on Christmas Eve. Church always was a part of our lives. I
inherited Christianity. A distant Christianity. It was something we
were to do. Without question. I had known the Methodist Church
since I was a child. I have heard the heavenly host in the hymns
from the choir loft. And the great organ-pipes like exhaust pipes
on transport trucks I have followed on highways and interstates.

The wise men came not in Luke, but in Matthew 2:1-12. They
brought frankincense, gold, and myrrh to finance the trip to
Egypt after Herod heard the King of the Jews had been born.

Sometimes I read Scripture and it passes. Other times it lands
with a clump. As when sections of snow fall from the roof to the
ground in a *whomp*. For years I lived in Minnesota shoveling the
walks and driveway. The silence. The austerity of snow. The roar
of wind above the house in a blizzard at night. It was as if there
was no ceiling, insulation, shingles, roof, or chimney to hold the
house in its yard. I stayed under the covers in the dark. My cat
against my back. I had wrapped her in her shawl until morning,
when we would go to the desk in my study.

Luke wrote his book with the message that the Gospels are delivered to us from those who were, from the beginning, eyewitnesses
and ministers of the word—and those who were prophets of the
Old Testament. "But thou, Bethlehem Ephratah, though thou be
little among the thousands of Judah, yet out of thee shall come forth
unto me that is to be ruler in Israel; whose goings forth have been
from of old, from everlasting" (Mic 5:2 KJV). Even the star in the
east bore witness that we might know the certainty (Lk 1:4 KJV).

I do not decorate much at Christmas because I usually am gone. Years ago, in Old Town Albuquerque, I purchased a small, flat tin Christmas tree with candleholders on the ends of the six branches and a seventh on top. There were decorative flowers pressed into the tin with petals in bas-relief. On the raised edges, I hanged a fat gold star. A pig in a wagon. A goose. A bell. A bird with a letter in its mouth. A Santa that must have been my husband's grand-mother's. A green felt tree sewn with sequins. Again his grand-mother's. A small paper cutout bear holding a basket my son drew and colored. A small card from a friend who died recently from Alzheimer's. A birch-bark deer.

"I have heard him, and observed him: I am like a green fir tree" (Hos 14:8 KJV).

Many in my family have passed. I am now the oldest one left. I travel between children and grandchildren at Christmas—between Kansas and Texas. A seven-and-a-half-hour journey. The few times I have been alone at Christmas, I feel the emptiness of the house, as heaven was empty of Christ during his years on earth, dying for my separation from heaven—but mainly for my distance from Christianity. But over the years, I have been in circumstances in which I needed a Savior. I have attended churches that preached the fundamental truth of Christ. That we are lost in a snowstorm without him. Our direction is confused, and we travel in circles unless he intercedes. He is the true chief. The way through. The Son of God. His majesty in power.

I have felt the transformation in my life. I had a tent dwelling, and he built a mansion so close to it I was subsumed into his house. He flooded my being. I have lived in a town that the highway cut through. I was displaced as I always have been displaced. But the road was Christ. I am a stranger on this earth (Ps 119:1 9KJV). A wayfarer. A sojourner. In the absolute poverty of my being, Christ was born so that in my wandering I carry an eternal home from which I will not have to depart.

The few times I light the small candles on the tin Christmas tree, they burn like stars in the east.

Tree at Christmas

MADELEINE L'ENGLE

The children say the tree must reach the ceiling.
And so it does, angel on topmost branch,
Candy canes and golden globes and silver chains,
Trumpets that toot, and birds with feathered tails.
Each year we say, each year we fully mean:
"This is the loveliest tree of all." This tree
Bedecked with love and tinsel reaches heaven.
A pagan throwback may have brought it here
Into our room, and yet these decked-out boughs
Can represent those other trees, the one
Through which we fell in pride, when Eve forgot
That freedom is man's freedom to obey
And to adore, not to replace the light
With disobedient darkness and self-will.
On Twelfth Night when we strip the tree
And see its branches bare and winter cold
Outside the comfortable room, the tree
Is then the tree on which all darkness hanged,
Completing the betrayal that began
With that first stolen fruit. And then, O God,
This is the tree that Simon bore uphill,
This is the tree that held all love and life.

Forgive us, Lord, forgive us for that tree.
But now, still decked, bedecked, in joy arrayed
For these great days of Christmas thanks and song,
This is the tree that lights our faltering way,
For when man's first and proud rebellious act
Had reached its nadir on that hill of skulls,
These shining, glimmering boughs remind us that
The knowledge that we stole was freely given
And we were sent the spirit's radiant strength
That we might know all things. We grasp for truth
And lose it till it comes to us by love.
The glory of Lebanon shines on this Christmas tree,
The tree of life that opens wide the gates.
The children say the tree must reach the ceiling
And so it does: for me the tree has grown so high
It pierces through the vast and star-filled sky.

Vigil: Christmas Eve, 1991

JOHN LEAX

From this dark wood, dormant
in star shine, the squirrels still in the bounty
of oak abundance,
the mice curled close beneath
the insulating snow,
nothing is far.

Here, above the valley,
in body-numbing cold I wait
to open what descends.
Nothing breaks over me.
Night is all. It holds me,
and lost in the loss
of sense, I ask nothing.

From the houses below
where friends dwell in peace
lights as steady as stars
rise to greet my watch.
No angel will descend.
All there is to see I see:
Christ is in his world.

In a Museum: To My Granddaughters

DAIN TRAFTON

These are the forms a painter made:
A father, a mother, and a child,
A broken wall and a distant town
Toward which a magpie flies alone,
Hay uncut in a level field.

These are the forms deeper than thought
That before all time, before dark and light,
God knew and in his knowing wrought:
The sharp-winged bird, the lonely town,
The wall undone, the field gone wild,
And redemption under a cracking sky,
A father, a mother, and a child.

Thursday, Day Twenty-Six

The Miracle of Sir Nick

LESLIE LEYLAND FIELDS

This is a dog story and also a Christmas story, but I will warn you up front, the ending is happy, but not quite, especially if you love dogs.

The dog's full name was Sir Nickolas Alexander. The pup was knighted shortly after birth by its twenty-something owner. The dog came through our doors unexpectedly that fall. I had four babies, one just a few weeks old, and the others older and louder and always up to mischief. After my son's birth, I had no idea how I could care for four little humans. And then came the dog. Surprise!

My husband, Duncan, was rescuing the dog, so the story went. Or rather, rescuing a young man. It was the strange-but-true case of a friend of a friend who was getting married, but his bride loved her dog (Sir Nickolas) more than her groom did. Friends staged an intervention shortly before the wedding, and we got the dog.

Nick was a beauty. He was a Sheltie, a miniature version of Lassie but fluffier and cuter. We imagined the kids romping with him in the living room. We expected the beautiful chaos of kids learning responsibility and palling around with their new best friend. But Nickolas wasn't interested in my children, or any of us. We tried repeatedly to capture his attention and his affection, but he was resolute. Ignoring an entire household can keep a dog busy, but Nickolas found other means of entertainment as well. He peed on my bed at least every week and ruined my Levolor blinds, but the worst habit was his frequent escape out the door to play in traffic. My furious neighbors called regularly, and animal control impounded him again and again, costing us big money to spring him. I was keenly disappointed with our new family member.

And I was struggling. My youngest was now two months old, and my eldest was seven years old. I was thankful to be down to just two nursings a night, but every day with my daughter and three sons was a marathon. One thing kept me going. As soon as I got the three-year-old and five-year-old safely down for a nap and then the baby snuggled in his crib, I ran to my bed and collapsed, breathing thanks-be-to-God in anticipation of a few moments of sleep. But this momentary quiet seemed to evoke his one great gift: barking.

I tried everything to make him happy and silent, but nothing seemed to work. Nor was my husband moveable. He liked the dog and wouldn't consider giving him away. Desperate, I spent "naptimes" devising humane ways to usher this dog out of my life. Then, as the weeks passed in a rising chorus of naptime soliloquies, not-so-humane. Until finally, two months later, near Christmas, utterly sleepless, I fell into imprecatory psalms and fervent prayers. I had never before prayed for the disappearance of any living thing. Why would God listen to such prayers? I felt foolish and guilty.

A week passed since my new prayers. This night was our school's Christmas program, to be held at our church. The elder two were in it, and one had a speaking part. We couldn't miss! We scurried around excitedly getting ready, but Duncan took sick. He remained in bed upstairs, knocked out with a stomach bug. Luckily I had help: a friend was visiting for the whole week, and this night, he was wrestling on the floor with Noah, five, while I put dinner away. Suddenly I heard, "Owwwww!" Ron was now flat on the carpeted floor, holding his jaw painfully. I ran to his side, and helped him up. He shuffled to the couch and sat down, all the while holding his jaw.

"What happened?" I asked, alarmed.

"My jaw. Noah hit it. It's out of place," he spoke, muffled, through his hand.

Ron was holding his jaw in pain; overhead, Duncan was noisily throwing up, the baby was crying, and we were supposed to be at the Christmas program in fifteen minutes. I stood paralyzed.

Then the doorbell rang. What? Who could it be?

I hurried to the door, wondering what could possibly happen next. I swung the door wide, then exclaimed, incredulously, "Jim! What are you doing here?" It was our friend who lived in Anchorage, a plane ride away. But we hadn't seen Jim for five years. Suddenly he's on our doorstep, tonight?

"I'm in Kodiak to go deer hunting. I thought I'd stop by and surprise you!" he smiled brightly. The best thing about Jim at that moment was not just that he was here at my door, but Jim was a dentist.

"Come in, quick! A friend just got his jaw knocked out of the socket. Can you help?"

He strode into the room, placed his hands on suffering Ron's face, made a few subtle movements, and soon Ron was sighing with relief.

I turned to Jim, astounded, when the doorbell rang again. What was going on here tonight?

I swung the door wide once more. It was my neighbor, Gretchen. Gretchen had two labs who terrorized me and my car every time I came and went. But something was wrong. Her face was white, and her eyes pinched and red.

"Leslie!" she said ominously, struggling for control.

"What? What happened?"

"I'm . . . I'm afraid it's Nick." She bit her lip.

"Nick?" I said, my voice rising.

"Yes. I'm afraid he was . . . he was hit by a car. I'm sorry. He's gone." She sucked in her breath, looking carefully at my face to make sure I was okay.

"Ohhhhhh my . . ." I stood frozen.

"He's . . . ummm, lying right near the turnout. I don't think he suffered." She sniffed and wiped her nose.

I don't know what my face looked like at that moment, but my heart was crackling with incredulity.

"Thank you so much for letting me know," I said slowly. I thanked her again and softly closed the door behind me.

Jim looked at me with concern. I didn't know how to feel. Our dog had just been killed. I had a house guest, a vomiting husband, a crying baby, a recovering friend, two kids to get to a Christmas program, and now a dead dog on my hands just minutes before the program started. (And a twinge of guilt through it all. Was it my prayers that did him in?)

And what about the kids? Do I tell them? The kids held little love for Nick, but I decided not to stir the night up any further. I would wait and tell them after the program. But what now?

Jim put a hand on my shoulder. "I've got this, Leslie. You go on to church, and I'll find the body and take care of him," he said kindly.

What? I blinked with wonder. I could have cried. I would cry later, alone, into my pillow as I relived these moments. In a few minutes we would go to our church to celebrate a God who came down as a babe to deliver his people. God-in-the-flesh who became God-on-the-cross to deliver us from sin and death. Isn't that enough, to rescue us from the jaws of death? But can it be, he also delivers his people from dislocated jaws? He delivers his people from sleepless days and errant dogs?

It is not quite the ending I wished or prayed for. Who does not mourn the death of any beautiful living thing? But the miracle is this. The dog did not come back to life, but *I did*. In a sleepless season of my life, God alone heard the prayers of an exhausted mother and came near, on a Christmas night, after a barreling car and a wandering dog, and in an angel of a man who flew in the nick of time to a faraway door to heal the sick and bury the dead.

God came that near. God came that far.

Is there *anyone* he cannot find?

Friday, Day Twenty-Seven

Melancholy Angels

PHILIP YANCEY

In my years of writing, I've not paid much attention to angels. I've never knowingly encountered one—knowingly, I say, for how could I tell for certain? Supernatural go-betweens, angels operate in the invisible world, rarely revealing themselves to those of us who occupy the material world.

I think of angels as something like the dark matter that physicists are still trying to understand. Our familiar world of matter—the Earth, stars and planets, everything that we can see—represents only 5 percent of the universe. Dark matter, which doesn't interact with "normal" matter, comprises some 27 percent, according to the latest estimates. We know dark matter exists due to its effect on gravitation but can't easily detect it since it doesn't absorb, reflect, or emit light.

Evidently angels have the ability to cross over between darkness and light, spanning the invisible and the visible worlds. They may act in subtle ways, through dreams, whispers, and mysterious coincidences—witness the many accounts of "guardian angel" experiences. Or, as in the biblical accounts, they may manifest themselves so dramatically that they must begin with the words "Fear not!"

As Christmas approaches, you can't avoid angels. They turn up in such places as Christmas carols in the mall, greeting cards, wrapping paper, nativity sets, and the tops of decorated trees. These cute, cuddly depictions have little in common with the angels of the Old Testament, who often came as warriors to dispense judgment.

Puzzled by this abrupt change in style, during Advent I took a closer look at the dozen accounts of angels in the four Gospels.

In the four centuries BC (notably, before Christ), Israel endured one humiliation after another as foreign empires invaded and devastated the land. God's people languished in a dark, cold spiritual winter with no prophets, no word from the Lord, and no apparent cross-overs from the supernatural world to give hope to the beleaguered.

Suddenly a flurry of angel visitations takes place. The archangel Gabriel announces the conception of John the Baptist to an old, barren couple, and an even more miraculous conception to a young woman named Mary. Joseph, who sorely needs reassurance, receives three different angelic visits. And in Bethlehem a host of angels fills the sky, dazzling a group of unsuspecting shepherds. At the birth of Jesus, an event of cosmic significance by which we humans still mark our calendars, the invisible and visible worlds come together.

Skip forward some three decades, and again angels are on the move. One with an appearance like lightning rolls away the stone that sealed Jesus' tomb, sending the guards into a state of stupor. Another (or were there two?) sits by the tomb informing a few women that Jesus is risen. "Tell his disciples *and Peter*," the angel commands, a poignant reminder that Jesus' most loyal disciple has betrayed him (Mk 16:7 NIV).

As I read these accounts, I can't help noticing the difference in demeanor between the multitude of angels who triumphantly announce Jesus' birth and the one or two angels *sitting* by the tomb carrying on a conversation. Gabriel struck Zechariah mute for his lack of faith, but the angels at the tomb seem oddly subdued. "Why do you look for the living among the dead?" they ask (Lk 24:5 NIV). As if wiser to the ways of this planet, they quote Jesus' own words about his predicted death. Not even the resurrection could erase the distress angels must have experienced during the time when God's own Son was brutalized by a mob of humans.

Besides the bevy of angels at Jesus' birth and resurrection, the Gospels record two other visitations, both at moments of Jesus' weakness. Angels ministered to him after the ordeal of Satan's temptation in the wilderness, when Jesus was famished and spiritually exhausted (Mt 4:11 NIV). And again, as Jesus faced the anguish of Gethsemane, with his companions sound asleep, an angel from heaven arrived to strengthen him (Lk 22:43 NIV). Luke, who recounted the dramatic appearances surrounding Jesus' birth, adds a postscript at the beginning of the book of Acts. Jesus gives a brief farewell address to the disciples, who are hoping for a glorious restoration of the kingdom to Israel. Instead, their leader commissions a new kind of kingdom, bestowing on them a mission to carry his message to the ends of the earth. Next, as they stand there slack-jawed, Jesus rises like a hot-air balloon and vanishes behind a cloud (Acts 1:6–11 NIV). In an almost comic scene, two angels ask, "Men of Galilee, why do you stand here looking into the sky?"—as if to say, "Didn't you hear what he said? It's up to you now, *so get going!*" They promise a future time when Jesus "will come back in the same way you have seen him go into heaven"— but not before the long, slow slog of history has run its course.

How do angels interact with the world now? The German director Wim Wenders offers one notion in his movie *Wings of Desire*, voted one of the best films of the 1980s. In it, two angels watch over the Cold War city of Berlin, unseen and unheard but still able to inspire thoughts and influence people: a pregnant woman in an ambulance, a young prostitute, a broken man contemplating suicide. Though powerful beings, the angels operate with surprising restraint and without overwhelming the humans' free will. Sometimes they fail, as in the case of the suicidal man who proceeds to jump off a building.

This Christmas season I've been reading the remarkable book *Wounded in Spirit* by David Bannon, which combines classic art with Advent meditations on grief. In its pages, I met the American artist Abbot Handerson Thayer, who died in 1921. Thayer seemed obsessed with angels, and his portraits have appeared on bookmarks, prints, and even the cover of *TIME* magazine. In this painting, Thayer used his twenty-seven-year-old daughter, Mary, as a model. The angel's melancholy expression reflects the sadness of the artist's life. Thayer lost one son at the age of two and another when the child was just three months old. His wife was institutionalized and died when Mary was fourteen.

Reading about Thayer's life, I reflected back on the angelic appearances in the Gospels and the limits of their power. Angels may surround us, invisibly, yet their activity on this planet is somehow constrained. An angel warned Joseph to flee to Egypt in order to escape Herod's massacre of the innocents but did not prevent the massacre itself. An angel strengthened Jesus at Gethsemane but did not prevent the crucifixion. Jesus himself declared, "Do you think I cannot call on my Father, and he will at once put at my disposal more than twelve legions of angels?" (Mt 26:53 NIV). He, too, felt constrained by the inevitability of history and his preordained sacrifice.

At Christmas, God subjected God's own self to the circumstances of a rebellious planet. Was not that the point of incarnation? A willing victim, Jesus joined us in a corner of the universe notorious for evil and suffering. According to the book of Hebrews, "In bringing many sons and daughters to glory, it was fitting that

God, for whom and through whom everything exists, should make the pioneer of their salvation perfect through what he suffered." The author later emphasizes that we now have a leader who can be touched with the feelings of our weaknesses (Heb 2:10; 4:15 NIV). God came alongside us in order to communicate divine love in the most effective way: human-to-human.

This season I also reread Dietrich Bonhoeffer's *Letters and Papers from Prison*. Writing to a friend, he describes Advent in prison as bombs fall and windowpanes shatter and fellow prisoners cry out in fear. "Life in a prison cell may well be compared to Advent; one waits, hopes, and does this, that, or the other—things that are really of no consequence—the door is shut, and can be opened only *from the outside*." Even so, he adds, faith can provide comfort in such times: "the calmness and joy with which we meet what is laid on us are as infectious as the terror that I see among the people here at each new attack. . . . We are neither of us dare-devils, but that has nothing to do with the courage that comes from the grace of God."

Unlike Peter's experience as recorded in Acts, no angelic messenger rescued Bonhoeffer. He died waiting and hoping; the Nazi SS executed him a few weeks before his prison camp was liberated. Bonhoeffer understood the constraints of power exercised from the bottom up, not from the top down. In one of his Christmas sermons, he says, "God is not ashamed of the lowliness of human beings. God marches right in. He chooses people as his instruments and performs his wonders where one would least expect them. God is near to lowliness; he loves the lost, the neglected, the unseemly, the excluded, the weak and broken."

At Christmas, God set aside the prerogatives of deity and joined us in our state of misery, opening the door *from the outside*, to free us for the day when we will join the angels in an unrestrained heavenly chorus.

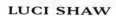

The Golden Ratio and the Coriolis Force*

LUCI SHAW

This morning God himself—his wafer—
lay for a moment naked on my tongue.
I felt the blood of God race through my veins.
Week by week Christ's flesh gets
broken down in my own body cells, as
the platelets in my plasma, like an uncurling
swirl of skyward birds, like my life spiral,
maintain their swift unwinding.

The second law.

The hurricanes, like commas
on the weather map. Amoebas.
Waterspouts. Curled fetuses.
Convolvulus vines twisting anti-clockwise
on the trellis. Dust devils dancing over fields.
The spiral nebulae. The nautilus.
The human ear. The bathtub water
scrolling down the drain—everything
made by God looks God-like,
and these unfolding spirals seem to me

the shape of God. The universe, once
wound up, is now rewinding, like my life—
to zero and the Everything of God
(who lay this morning naked
on the manger of my tongue).

---

*The Coriolis force describes how moving objects, as water going down a drain, are deflected as a result
of the Earth's rotation, spiraling right in the Northern Hemisphere and left in the Southern Hemisphere.

The Forest Primeval

PAUL WILLIS

I am five years old. It is a lamentable
week—or two weeks—after Christmas in Anaheim.
All the way around the block there are
Christmas trees at mute attention on the curb.
They are stripped of lights and stars and angels,
and lean against the garbage cans with only a trace
or two of tinsel, tawdry in the morning light.

These trees are lonely, I decide. They need
to be brought together somewhere to commiserate,
to regain a semblance of miracle. Somewhere
like my backyard. One by one, on a rescue mission,
I drag them down the sidewalk and around our house
and plant them one against the other, a thick
entangling of grateful boughs. All afternoon

I crawl inside their fragrant shade, touching open
pockets of pitch and feeling needles rain down
softly in my hair. The trees are happy to be so close.
They recall what it was like to flourish in peace, to offer
their presence, young as they are, an ancient grove.
It is a delight to have them here, in my backyard, here
where we will grow together for many years,
where I will always be the gift beneath these trees.

Part Three

Jesus in Us for the World

It is the third part of our anthology, "Jesus in Us for the World," that reaches beyond what might be expected in a group of readings for Advent. Jesus is born to be born in us, and he is born in us for a reason: that we might bear his presence and impart his goodness, imperfect as we remain.

"Christ is in his world," declared John Leax, and that is true, whether in far flung galaxies that Madeleine L'Engle glimpses in her imagination or in the homely white-faced steer that Benjamin Myers flatly encounters, "its hooves in muck."

As human beings made and redeemed in God's image, however, "We are meant and designed to be light bearers and agents of love." Those are the words of Marilyn McEntyre, richly borne out by many of the writers that follow—Sarah Arthur in her wrenching encounters with the homeless; Jeanne Murray Walker in her teaching visits with women prisoners; Deborah Dickerson in her simple, straightforward sharing of daily bread with her neighbors. All to be done in gentleness, as her husband Matthew reminds us. Or, as Amanda Lee Devos Newell puts it, soft as the cry of an owl in the dark.

Sunday, Day Twenty-Nine

You Come, Too

MARILYN McENTYRE

Advent, from *advenire*,
"to come to." A time to remember
who came, and to whom.

A shock of starlight
divided the night sky
in the dead of winter

to mark that coming. He arrived
who was already here—still arrives—
advenit, bidden or unbidden,

to those who lie awake, to children
who dress as shepherds and small angels
in sheets who forget their lines,

to guests who gather
at laden tables, and lean ones,
and on the darkest night

in the unbearable loneliness
of fresh loss. *Advenit*—he comes
to each, to all of us. Ritually

we await what is here, already
but not yet, in sure and certain hope
of things not seen except

through a darkened glass. Angels
hover, the Spirit passes and a flame
flickers, faces brighten and every

baby's eyes look like God's.
All that arrives in Advent reminds us:
we are met in the midst of the night,

dormant and chill, by one who
comes and dwells among us, waiting, too.
He listens, we listen, and silence is sanctified.

Advenit—he comes—again and always.
And so we summon one another in hope and song:
Venite adoremus. You come, too.

Piano

PAUL WILLIS

The summer you were seven
you could hardly sleep
that night before your first recital.
I'd rather break my arm, you said.

Which is what you did with an hour
to spare. We could blame the dog
who chased you into the glass door,
but that would be dumb. A wish,

you found, is a dangerous thing.
Today, eight years old and nearly
Christmas, you asked to be the first
on the program. As you sat waiting,

sunlight fell on the bowl-cut line
behind your head. Sometimes
just a year is enough to learn
to bring joy to the world.

✳ Shine ✳

GINA OCHSNER

His word is in my heart like a fire, like a fire shut up in my bones.
I am weary of holding it in; indeed, I cannot.

JEREMIAH 20:9 NIV

O nce, a boy fell in love with fire. It happened in the usual way. One winter morning his mother built a roaring blaze in their little grate, and from that moment on, the boy was smitten. Although the mother did not have strong eyes, the boy did, and he loved to look at the dancing flames. He loved how they were blue at the bottom, then turned yellow and orange. He could sit for over an hour staring at those flames, studying them as if he were reading his life's future.

The boy would be sitting there now, still staring at those flames, had not three things happened. First, the boy's grandfather, a person about whom he knew very little, fell gravely ill. The boy and his mother, along with a vast assortment of relatives, neighbors, and friends, went to visit the old man.

There inside the old man's home was an enormous pot-bellied stove, bigger than any stove the boy had seen before. This stove was the second thing, not just because of its great size or the way it wobbled a little on its iron legs, as if the fire frizzling and snapping inside of it made it dance. What drew the boy's interest to the stove was the great quantity of coals in the stove's iron belly, and the way the iron stove had turned cherry red from the heat.

As the boy and his mother passed the pot-bellied stove, a low cough rumbled from a room no bigger than a broom closet. Inside, the boy's grandfather lay small and crumpled in a bed pushed next to the wall. On this wall hung a poster for a traveling circus. This poster was the third thing, because near the bottom, ringed in a circle of fire, was a photo of the boy's grandfather when he was a much younger man. In the picture the young man had a handlebar mustache and his face glowed with a strange interior light. Written beneath the photo were the words "Mircea the Great: Eater of Unquenchable Fires." This was how the boy discovered that his grandfather was in love with fire too.

"Come here, my boy." The grandfather's voice flaked like bits of ash floating on hot air. But his face glowed and eyes shone with a fierce light.

The boy leaned over his grandfather, carefully pressing his cheek next to his grandfather's bristly ashen one. "What is the secret of fire-eating?" the boy asked. Like an ember over which a small gust of air passes, the old man's eyes brightened. "Love," he rasped, and his voice smelled like a dry scorched wind.

Then the grandfather's gaze traveled from one family member to the next and finally settled on a wiry-looking man who was not part of the family or a neighbor. The man looked very much like the boy's grandfather: the skin on the backs of his hands and neck was creased like a wallet that had been opened and closed many, many times. He had no eyebrows, as if they'd been scorched.

But his face shone as if he'd swallowed a lantern. He wore blue trousers made of silk that had thin gold piping down the sides. It was clear that at one time these trousers had been very fine, though the boy could tell from the shine on the knees and the cuffs how very worn (well-loved, his mother might say) they really were.

"I'm hot," the boy's grandfather said to the old man in the blue trousers. The man shuffled to the kitchen, found a glass, filled it with water, and gave it to the boy's grandfather. The man drank the water, smiled, then closed his eyes. And then the boy's grandfather was gone, as if the water had extinguished him.

As the friends, family, and neighbors filed solemnly through the kitchen and past the cherry red pot-bellied stove, the man in the blue trousers gave each of them an empty tin of sprats. Where there should have been sprats there was instead a single coal taken from the clattering pot-bellied stove.

"He would have wanted you all to have some of his fire," the old man said to each of the friends, relatives, and neighbors as he gave them a tin. But to the boy he whispered: "This coal is special. Don't let it go out."

From that day forward the boy's mother was careful not to talk too much about the boy's famous fire-eating grandfather. She wanted her son to take up other hobbies, like football or chess or classical Spanish guitar, because it seemed these days that the world had little use for what seemed like strange and irrelevant passions such as taming lions, walking wires, or even eating fire.

But it was no good. The boy was consumed with the idea of eating fire just as his grandfather the Great Mircea had done.

The boy kept the coal burning and from it he lit matches and candles and cigars. And these he practiced swallowing morning, noon, and night. If his mother put a book before him he would tear the pages out one by one, set them on fire, and swallow them. Many fine and worthy books were consumed in this manner.

The boy didn't have a lot of friends, only acquaintances who lived in the same building as he did and who went to the same school. They weren't impressed by the boy's unusual talents.

"Who cares about fire," said one tallish boy who had always been a torment to every other boy younger and smaller than himself. "My grandpa knew a man who could walk twenty kilometers on his hands. My grandmother knew a woman who trained her cats to pluck at a mandolin. Are you going to swallow fire while you walk on your hands or have trained cats pluck at a mandolin?"

The boy merely shrugged his shoulders. It hadn't yet occurred to him that consuming fire would seem ordinary to other people. "I'm still in training," he said at last, and he struck a match against the building, flicked it into the air where it turned in circles. Then he caught the match on his tongue. If it stung, the boy didn't let on. He was still puzzling over his grandfather's piece of advice: love. What did love have to do with fire?

* * *

Day and night the boy practiced. It was probably a good thing his mother didn't have keen eyesight: she might have worried if she could have seen the quantity of sharp and blazing items that he tossed into the air and passed behind his back and between his legs. She might have watched as he put lighted taper after taper down his throat, where, *poof!* out they went. She might have seen his keen disappointment at what seemed to him his complete failure.

"Mother," the boy said one day, "I practice and practice, but I don't get any better." And his voice could not have been any more crumpled or small.

The mother squinted at her boy. She understood his frustration. From her own girlhood attempts to eat fire, she knew that it was one thing to hold fire in your mouth. It is quite another to hold it in your belly and send it leaping back out again.

She put one hand on each of her son's shoulders. "You have done all that a boy with some talent can do. Now you must visit your grandfather's apprentice. Oh—and take that coal with you."

Deep in the heart of a vast concrete forest, the apprentice lived in a tiny hut. Tall apartment buildings loomed on every side, casting long shadows over his hut. This was, in part, why the apprentice had grown to love fire almost as much as Mircea the Great had. Fire produced light that scattered those long shadows. And fire produced heat that drew the coldness out of his bones.

Sure, with fire came hazards: twice he'd almost burned down his kitchen, and soot lined his wrinkles and the walls of his little house. He had a lingering cough and a general impatience split evenly between people who carelessly set a fire and those who snuffed a flame when they had no reason to. This was why he wouldn't allow anyone into his tiny hut until they answered a few questions.

The boy knocked on the apprentice's door. With his dark hair and a thin down of dark hair above his upper lip that with care might someday be groomed into a handlebar mustache, the boy looked so like the Mircea the Great that the apprentice was stunned for a moment. Then he barked:

"Do you love fire?"

"Yes," said the boy.

"Did you bring a coal burning hot and fierce?"

"Yes," said the boy.

The small door slowly swung open on rusty hinges.

The boy recognized the apprentice. He was the same old man with leathery looking skin who had been at his grandfather's apartment. He was wearing the blue trousers that shone at the knees.

The apprentice pointed to the kitchen where a stove sat humming and crackling with a stout fire. A bright bed of coals smoldered beneath the flames. "Something you should know about fire," the apprentice lifted a finger in the air. "It consumes what it loves. Watch this." The apprentice lifted a glass to his lips. The glass was full of liquid the color of fish oil. The apprentice drank it in one gulp. Then he lit a match, opened his mouth, tossed the match inside. The apprentice opened his mouth wide, wide. A jet of orange fire blazed from his mouth and scorched a swath of carpet.

"I'm afraid," the boy said so suddenly he seemed to surprise himself with his own words.

"Good," the apprentice smiled. "You should be." He rubbed his dry hands together and the boy thought he saw a little spark fly out from between the man's palms. "Now it's your turn. Show me what you know how to do."

And so the boy showed the apprentice all the tricks he'd mastered. But it was as before, the moment the flame touched the inside of his mouth or tongue, it fizzled out.

"What am I doing wrong?" the boy asked.

The apprentice tipped his head and nodded at the boy's tin. "You forgot to swallow the coal. The coal keeps all other fires lit."

Now, why hadn't I thought of that before? the boy wondered. And then on the heels of that question was a more pressing one: "Will it hurt?" the boy asked.

"No more than anything else does," the apprentice said as he handed the boy a glass filled with the liquid that looked like fish oil. The boy understood what he needed to do: he drank the liquid, then balanced the coal on his tongue as if it were a pill from a doctor's clinic. Then he tipped his head back and swallowed it whole. It burned terribly as it travelled down his throat and settled in the pit of his stomach.

The apprentice peered at him carefully. "How do you feel?"

"Warm."

"Good. Swallow another." The apprentice pointed to the bed of coals in the stove.

And so the boy did.

"How do you feel?"

"Warmer."

"Good."

And this went on and on for hours until the boy's belly could hold no more coals and the apprentice sent the boy home. As he walked home, the boy felt not a particle of pain, not an ounce of discomfort. He merely felt warm, from the pit of his stomach to the crown of his head.

And something else: in the reflection of the many glass windows he passed, he saw that his face had changed. His face was acquiring a glow not at all unlike that of his grandfather's.

As he trundled up the stairwell of his apartment building, the boy encountered the tallish boy, the one who had teased him. The tallish boy could not help but notice how the boy's face shone like a beacon or the otherworldly confidence about the boy as he strode past him and up the stairs. It was so very strange that the tallish boy could not think of a single insult to hurl in the boy's direction.

His mother, however, was overjoyed at the sight of her son all aglow. For starters, with her poor eyesight, she'd never been able to see him as clearly as now, and she could see how very happy he was. For the apprentice had been right: the right coal lodged in the right place fires all fire. As long as the boy took care not to douse the coals, he could swallow fire and send it back out of his mouth as much as he liked.

Walls being what they are in such apartment buildings—that is, thin—it didn't take long for all the neighbors to hear about the boy's transformation. And the boy, so excited about his new skills, couldn't help but juggle fiery sticks and insert them into his open mouth and withdraw them, still flaming. This delighted the very young. But it horrified the elderly who, in principle, devote as

much time and energy as possible into dampening any such sights
or news of sights they might find potentially shocking.

And times were different. It was a different sort of a world the
boy lived in, very different from the day of Mircea the Great
where oddities and strangeness were embraced, heralded, revered.

"It's not natural," said one elderly woman who often said this of
anything she did not understand.

"It can't be healthy," said the superintendent to the boy's mother.
"He should see someone about this. Professionally."

The mother shook her head. "This is what he's meant for, what
he's made to do and be."

This was all fine and well while the light was a novelty, but after
some time the residents of the apartment building had enough.
They could not look at the boy without getting a headache.

"Why not wear sunglasses?" The boy's mother suggested to
anyone who complained. The truth was, she liked how her son
turned her darkness to light. She did not mind keeping a roaring
fire in the grate so that he could eat coals whenever he felt the need.

Of course the simple solution for the boy: stop eating fire. But
once you've tasted it, it becomes you. You never want to feel cold
again. You never want to live in darkness.

The second solution, and this the tallish boy thought up all by
himself: douse the boy and thus, douse the light. This he proposed
to do with a large bucket and a hose.

And the tallish boy attempted this one morning as the boy
passed in the stairwell. But the moment the water touched the boy,
it sizzled and evaporated into scalding steam. The tallish boy tried
again, several days in a row, but the fact of the matter was no one
had water wet enough to quench the burning boy.

"Well, it will not do to have a boy walking around like a beacon,
like a living lamppost. It will upset and disturb other boys who

may try to imitate him," a neighbor who had several boys of her own said.

"It's very dangerous," an elderly tenant agreed.

"Give a boy a match or a candle or a lighter and the trouble is sure to follow," said another.

But they could not separate the boy from the fire or the fire from the boy. In fact, it seemed as the days went by that he was actually glowing brighter.

"This will not do." The neighbors cornered the mother and her beaming boy. "It is unfair that the abnormalities of the one should inconvenience the many." It was by the words they used, the formality of them, and the flat, atonal way they said them, as if the words themselves suggested distance, that the woman understood that she and her boy would have to do something right away.

Early the next morning the boy and his mother left the apartment building. Of course, because the boy's face was aglow, brighter than a freshly scrubbed moon, the neighbors could see quite clearly what was happening. And they sighed in relief. They'd get some sleep at last; they'd not be bothered by light where they did not want it. And the strangeness of a boy with coals swilling in his belly and a face alight with an unquenchable fire would dim as these things do in time, until the boy faded to a rattling packet of words, a bit of a fairy tale the elderly told their grandchildren to scare them.

But on cloudless evenings when the fogs lifted their skirts, if those grandchildren were to look to the hills they might see a light, small but certain. You can still see it from time to time.

✳ I Was Thirsty ✳

✳

When he finally arrives, blazing in beauty and all his angels with him, the Son of Man will take his place on his glorious throne. Then all the nations will be arranged before him and he will sort the people out, much as a shepherd sorts out sheep and goats, putting sheep to his right and goats to his left.

"Then the King will say to those on his right, 'Enter, you who are blessed by my Father! Take what's coming to you in this kingdom. It's been ready for you since the world's foundation. And here's why:

I was hungry and you fed me,
I was thirsty and you gave me a drink,
I was homeless and you gave me a room,
I was shivering and you gave me clothes,
I was sick and you stopped to visit,
I was in prison and you came to me.'

"Then those 'sheep' are going to say, 'Master, what are you talking about? When did we ever see you hungry and feed you, thirsty and give you a drink? And when did we ever see you sick or in prison and come to you?' Then the King will say, 'I'm telling the solemn truth: Whenever you did one of these things to someone overlooked or ignored, that was me—you did it to me'" (Matthew 25:34-43).

How Are You, My Friend?

PAUL WILLIS

For the year after our house burned down in a wildfire, my wife and I rented a condominium near downtown Santa Barbara. Our block was a mix of gentrified complexes and broken-down old homes. The street was shaded, the sidewalks buckled, and parking difficult to find. The condo had a roomy, covered front porch from which we could watch motorcycles motor by, but I don't recall that we sat down on that front porch all that often. Something about the trauma of the fire kept us restlessly pacing.

Our son was just a year out of college and back home from Los Angeles to work in a law office a few blocks away. A lover of cars, he had just bought a used Audi wagon to haul his drums from gig to gig. The perfect set of wheels for that purpose, he said. Our daughter lived a couple miles away with some friends, finishing up her own last year of college. This was our family—not counting the dog, which counted for a lot in those days. Years before, just after the 9/11 attacks, I took our dog to school for a week so the students could pet him during class. Similarly, in that year after the fire, our dog got a lot of attention. Or we craved his.

Right behind our condo was an old corner grocery store that had just been taken over by an immigrant family from Syria. It had become more of a liquor store, actually. The grocery part was fairly sad. The bananas were speckled, the ice cream was chalky, and the milk perpetually past date. It was the kind of grocery store we only went to when we needed something at the last minute. But in the evening I would often walk the dog past the store and find the aging Syrian proprietor sitting calmly on the sidewalk, firing up a little stove to make some tea. Every time I walked by, he would call out, "How are you, my friend?"

I would say that I was fine and continue on.

The proprietor had two sons who worked in shifts. They were about the age of my own. Unlike their father, they were full of hurry and energy, as if through sheer force of personality their shabby corner grocery store could become the next Walmart. I often thought of them growing old in the fierce white light of those bottles of vodka behind the counter, their nimble hands passing change for packs of gum and packs of condoms. I wished that my students had half their hurry and energy; I wished that these two Syrian boys could go to college.

Late one spring evening, five months after the fire, our daughter woke us up with a call: our son had been in an accident in his Audi wagon. A very bad accident. He was in the emergency room, and we should get there, right away. When we found him there, propped up in a bed and no longer conscious, he was still bleeding badly from a depressed skull fracture. He would need immediate surgery. Friends gathered through the night as he lay on the operating table, and then, in the morning, came word of likely recovery.

I do not remember everything of the weeks that followed, but here is something I do remember. My wife stayed at the hospital for several days and nights running, and I went home from time to time to walk the dog. One evening the dog and I passed in front of the corner grocery, and there was the old proprietor, sitting calmly on the sidewalk, firing up his stove for tea.

"How are you, my friend?" he said.

I stopped this time. I could not say I was fine, for I was not fine. Suddenly this Syrian man seemed to me the friendliest presence on the planet. I approached, and he very graciously arose. I told the dog to sit. And then I told the man about my son and his accident, about his crushed skull, and his operation, and how in the morning he had quietly opened his eyes and spoken to us. A miracle. But I told him how worried we were still, how the outcome was in no way sure, how my wife was still at the hospital and here I was, walking the dog.

The Syrian man stood very quietly and nodded. He listened to every word I said. "That is very hard, my friend," he said.

And then he said, "Please. Some tea, my friend."

I'd like to think I accepted his offer, that he poured me some tea in a little cracked cup, that we sat quietly side by side and drank together in little sips. But I probably just thanked him and left.

Night after night, however, I came back, walking the dog. And every time I passed by, if the Syrian father was sitting by the purr of his stove, he would call out, "How is your son, my friend?"

And I would tell him. Whatever the news might be, I would tell him. And my heart would well, every time. My heart, that little cracked cup.

Christmas and the Cross

LAUREN F. WINNER

Luke 1 and 2 are often described as "the Lukan infancy and childhood narratives"—the stories of Jesus' birth and early childhood. That description is fine, but as Eugene Peterson has suggested, there is another way of framing the opening of Luke: these two chapters are a primer in prayer. Prayers saturate the first two chapters of Luke. Practically the entire story of Jesus' birth is told in prayers—in the *Fiat mihi* ("Let it be to me according to your will"), Mary announces her acceptance of God's will; in the Magnificat ("My soul glorifies the Lord"), she praises God for turning things upside down and inside out.

The next prayer is spoken by Zechariah, the husband of Mary's cousin, Elizabeth. He has been struck mute for months. On the day that his son John is named and circumcised, Zechariah finally gets his speech back. In that situation, my first words might be curses. But Zechariah's first words are words of prayer: "Praise be to the Lord, the God of Israel, because he has come and has redeemed his people." Then comes a prayer that is very familiar to us at Christmastime—the Gloria: in the wake of Jesus' birth, a chorus of angels sings "Glory to God in the highest, and peace to his people on earth." Today, we repeat that prayer, which praises God and declares God's will for peace.

Finally, in verses 29-32 of Luke 2, we get the prayer now known as the *Nunc Dimittis*:

> Lord, you now have set your servant free
> to go in peace as you have promised;
> For these eyes of mine have seen the Savior,
> whom you have prepared for all the world to see:
> A light to enlighten the nations,
> and the glory of your people Israel.

Praying this prayer at bedtime as we sometimes do, we risk domesticating what is really a quite remarkable and unsettling scene. It is unsettling not only because Simeon is announcing his readiness to die. He is also alerting Mary to Jesus' death: "A sword will pierce your own soul too." Here he is predicting her suffering, and, by extension, he is suggesting Jesus' suffering, since it is the piercing of Jesus' side that will pierce her. Simeon's opaque and poetic line, in other words, is a subtle instruction to remember the cross.

Remember the cross at Christmas? Aren't we supposed to think about the cross on Good Friday, and the manger, homely and sweet, today? Actually, remembering the cross is part of the adult version of Christmas. Let's face it; Christmas is a time of great happiness, but it is also, for many of us, a time of great struggle. At Christmastime, some of us count up all the people we loved who have died, and we yearn for them. Some of us feel hideously lonely, and our loneliness seems all the more glaring because it's out of sync with the script of seasonal happiness we think we're supposed to be following. We are not alone in this suffering. Mary, our text hints, was suffering on Jesus' behalf, in anticipation of Jesus' later suffering.

Simeon's reminder of Jesus' suffering and our suffering brings us back to prayer. We are called into a life in which God, in response to our suffering, breaks into the world, and that in-breaking is accompanied by God's own suffering (and the suffering of God's mother, Mary). We heed Jesus' call into a suffering life by prayer. Prayer, after all, is the place where we enter into one another's suffering, and where God draws near to our suffering. It is also the place where we participate in God's comfort and in God's redemption of our suffering—and this baby Jesus does not conquer the powerful with the sword, but by living a life of suffering and prayer, and by dying.

Over and over throughout the first two chapters of Luke, God's faithful people respond to God by praying. I take two larger insights about prayer from these praying faithful. First, prayer is the channel through which we participate in God's breaking into the world. Second, prayer is not a hard task that we have to initiate. Rather, our prayer, like the prayers of Mary, Zechariah, the angelic choir and Simeon, is a response to the work that God is already doing. This is part of the good news of the *Nunc Dimittis*—God enters into our lives not just by being born two thousand years ago, but by constituting a community of praying people that includes an unmarried teenage girl who is pregnant and an elderly man who is on his last legs. And just as that teenage girl and that old man enter God's story through proclamations of faithfulness and praise, so too God enters our lives by inviting us to enter into God's life through prayer.

A Welcome-Unwelcome Traveler in Narnia

MATTHEW DICKERSON

Let your gentleness be evident to all. The Lord is near.

PHILIPPIANS 4:5 NIV

The Lion, the Witch and the Wardrobe* begins as a Christmas story. At the start, we learn that Narnia is suffering under the dreadful power of the White Witch, who makes it always winter and never Christmas. Then into the Narnia tale comes the creator incarnate in the person of Aslan to rescue his creation from slavery and the power of death. The other six books in The Chronicles of Narnia powerfully display the effects of that incarnation. Throughout the books, Lewis suggests that Christ is in us through our practice of gentleness.

For more than thirty years I have been teaching seminar-style writing classes for first-year students at Middlebury, a small liberal arts college in Vermont where I am a professor. I'll teach a class on Lewis for a couple years, then switch over and teach J. R. R. Tolkien's works for a while, and then switch back to Lewis. Middlebury is a secular institution, and few of my students—even in my C. S. Lewis classes—are followers of Christ. Before the start of the semester, my students are often familiar with Lewis only as the author of The Chronicles of Narnia. Knowing that most of my students didn't come from church backgrounds, I was curious one year to see what portrayals or scenes of Aslan were most compelling for them or moved them most deeply.

For two consecutive years, the answer I received from the non-Christian students in my classes was almost universal. It was not Aslan on the Stone Table giving his life to save others that my students found most compelling. Nor was it Aslan roaring into battle or showing up in power to save the day as he does toward the end of The Lion, the Witch and the Wardrobe or in Prince Caspian. Neither is it the un-dragoning of Eustace in The Voyage of the Dawn Treader (although that is one of my own favorite scenes) or even the singing of Narnia into being in The Magician's Nephew. These are all powerful, moving scenes for many fans of Lewis's writings.

Yet for the vast majority of my students at Middlebury College, the most compelling portrayal of Aslan in all the Chronicles is when he appears to a lonely, lost, discouraged Shasta—who at the time considers himself "the most unfortunate boy that ever lived in the whole world"—in The Horse and His Boy. Here we see the great lion as a comforter. He is quiet, present, and listening. For a long while, he simple walks beside Shasta, his presence made evident only through the sound of his breath or in a "deep, rich sigh out of the darkness beside him."

When Shasta asks, "Who are you?" Aslan replies in a quiet voice, "One who has waited long for you to speak." And then, shortly, he breathes on Shasta and says to him, "Tell me your sorrows."

My students longed for gentleness, even if they didn't have a name for it, and even if our culture does not value it.

It's easy for Christians to think that a message of hellfire and damnation will lead people to salvation. Or perhaps we believe that demonstrations of power in politics or wealth will win or coerce people into God's kingdom. Paul writes something different in Romans 2:4 NIV: "Or do you show contempt for the riches of his kindness, forbearance and patience, not realizing that God's kindness is intended to lead you to repentance?"

Wait. What? It's God's kindness that leads people to him? That sounds a whole lot like gentleness. In fact, the word Paul uses in Romans is one that can also be translated as "gentleness."

I'm particularly moved by Paul's exhortation toward gentleness in Philippians 4:5 NIV: "Let your gentleness be evident to all. The Lord is near." He puts gentleness all alone in this phrase as a virtue to be practiced, placing a special emphasis on it. If you go into a grocery store with a long shopping list, it's easy to forget an item, no matter how important it might be. If you have just one item on the list, you give it special attention; it's not forgotten. Gentleness is a virtue to be singled out. Pay attention to it.

Gentleness is not merely a feeling, but something that should be evident to those around us. It shouldn't be hidden away. And surely we need to be gentle not just toward a few chosen select people, but with everybody: with those outside the church, and those within our church community; with our friends, and with those we may consider our enemies; with our family, and with our colleagues at work. And, even when we encounter the rude driver at the traffic light, and the customer service representative at the airline terminal after a long wait in line when our flight has been canceled.

Paul follows this injunction with four simple words: "The Lord is near." This isn't a threat, like the notion of Santa Claus who is always watching to see if you've been bad or good. We should hear in those words the profoundly encouraging message that Christ is in us. Gentleness is not the fruit of our self-effort, but the fruit of the Spirit's transformational work in our lives. "God is near," Paul reminds his readers. "He will help you to be gentle if you let him."

Reading this passage from *The Horse and His Boy* again, with tears welling in my own eyes, I think of a similarly discouraged and exhausted Elijah. It was not in the powerful wind that the prophet Elijah heard God. It was not in the earthquake or fire either; rather, it was in "a gentle whisper" that God spoke to Elijah. So, too, did God speak to the students in my C. S. Lewis class through the gentle whisper of Aslan.

And so, too, does God speak to the world today, through the gentleness of those who follow him.

Advent

BENJAMIN MYERS

At 4:00 it's getting dark. Thin fog
picks dead leaves from a lone hackberry tree
and drops them on the yellowed grass. Our dog
noses the dead wet leaves and twig debris,

which flushes out a burst of quail to try
to break the seal between the earth and sky.

The Book of Nature

BENJAMIN MYERS

I can't believe that nature ever speaks
    when I am looking at a white-faced steer,
        its hooves in muck, the rain nipping its back,
a wad of winter grass working its cheeks.
    I can't believe there's anything to hear
        in that dumb stare, in that four-gutted sack.

But hearing and what speaks are not the same.
    A voice calls out loudly but not near.
        And, since I've walked so far into the black,
I'll need to note the unheard voice and name
        the lack.

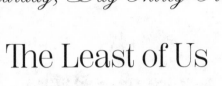

The Least of Us

SARAH ARTHUR

He looks, at first glance, like any ordinary white college student. Backpack slung over one shoulder, hipster-esque brown hair, slight build, hesitant demeanor. I only notice him in the crowd at Chicago's Union Station because he's now approached three people in the waiting area, voice too low to hear. All I see are their quick headshakes, the clipped "no"s on lips, the averted glances. He nods respectfully after each encounter, then shuffles away in a new loop around the building.

I'm here on business, four hours from home. I've missed my connection to the western suburbs; I'm frantically rifling through a folder, trying to find contact info for the publisher I'm supposed to meet in one hour. I've crammed my phone in the crook of my shoulder and my various bags under my arms and legs, and I'm about as convincingly unapproachable as a traveling professional can be. But I know he's coming my way. Before I actually see him again, I sense the advance of the child of some brokenhearted woman in Wilmette or Elmhurst or Wheaton, and I steel myself for what I have to say. This week, it will be the millionth time I've told a child "no."

A child. Some mother's son. And he must sense that I'm some son's mother because he angles cautiously into my line of sight.

"I'm sorry to bother you," he says in the quiet rasp of a ruined voice, "but I accidentally left my wallet on the bus, and I need money for a train ticket home."

Up close I can see the dirt, the split upper lip, the unsteady vision. God, he can't be more than eighteen. My kindergartner in, oh, twelve years. What kind of hell did he sleep in last night? What kind of hell did his mother sleep in?

I know from experience how this conversation goes. I will say, "I'm happy to buy you a ticket, but I can't give you money." And he'll say some variation of, "I won't catch a train right away, so really, a couple dollars for a sandwich while I wait . . ." And then I'll say, firmly, "I have a granola bar and a cheese stick right here." But by then the game will be up.

I suddenly miss my two little boys with an ache like mild electrocution. I look him in the eyes. I want him to see that I see him. I want him to know that he is known—if not by me, then by a God who, like a mother, knows us. All our desires, longings, addictions, agonies . . . all of it.

I decide to short-circuit the script. "I'm sorry, honey," I say, as if one of my sons has just asked for candy that will ruin his teeth; "I can't do that." Instead I want to throw my body between him and the train that is barreling through his system, the addiction that likely will end his life. I want to ask, "Does your mother know where you are?" I want to flag down a nurse, drive him to the hospital, hold vigil by the driplines and the blinking monitors, my life on pause till he takes an honest breath again. Everything his mother probably wants to do but can't, because, at the end of all things, we don't get to save our children. We don't get to save anyone.

✳ ✳ ✳

If I've learned nothing else in the past fifteen years of inviting the homeless to live with my family, it's that we're not here to fix the world. It's tempting to believe otherwise, especially for someone steeped in an evangelical milieu that began at Christian summer camps and concerts, continued through a flagship Christian college in the Chicago suburbs, and drifted, rather unremarkably, by slow oxbows, back to my mainline roots in Michigan. Evangelicals are the great hope of the world, we're told. We have the good news. We're here to change your life. No, wait, sorry: we get ourselves confused with Jesus *all the time.*

I wasn't raised liberal or conservative, theologically speaking. I was raised in a kind of "generous orthodoxy," to quote author Brian McLaren (who was paraphrasing theologian Hans Frei). We adhered to the ancient Christian creeds—with high views of Jesus, the Bible, and the church—but we didn't turn a deaf ear to other ways of being Christian, or religious, or even spiritual. Who were we to foreclose on how God chooses to engage the world? We were otherwise socially conservative—with the exception of a strange discontent in my bones about justice. Something bigger than personal sin was at stake in the problems I kept seeing in the world. Entire systems were egregiously stacked against the most vulnerable. Systemic sin. Sin that's greater than the sum of its individual parts.

In college, this discontent took the form of weekly ministry to children in the projects on Chicago's south side and spending a semester feeding and playing with hungry kids in the slums of Nairobi, Kenya. I met my future husband through an inner-city ministry, both of us recognizing that here was someone whose understanding of sin was both personal and communal. *We sin.* Not just me. Not just you. Us, together. And the solution is more involved than simply laying all those personal sins at the foot of the cross (pardon the Christianese) and moving on, knowing you've been forgiven. It's a group project, requiring actual strategies for systemic change: in churches, in agencies, in programs and policies. And in homes.

At its core, how we learn to engage the world starts with the nuclear family and its posture toward those outside. Somehow, even as newlyweds, my husband and I understood this. Shortly after we moved into our first house in a small Michigan town, we invited a man from the local homeless shelter—where my husband volunteered monthly—to live with us. Because somewhere in our Bible training, Jesus' parable of the sheep and the goats in Matthew 25:45 sounded like a blueprint for setting up a house, setting up a life. "Whatever you've done for the least of these [the stranger, the hungry, thirsty, sick, imprisoned], you've done for me," Jesus tells his followers. Feed the hungry, and you're feeding Jesus. Our main guy.

So, we invited Jesus to live with us. We asked a stranger to join our household, to eat at our table, to become family. And it didn't take long before I realized this wasn't a program or policy or plan. This was a person. He had his quirks; he could be a pain in the ass. But so could I. And if we were going to survive, we needed to learn to mutually respect each other without the ever-evasive goal of trying to fix another human being. Because you can't.

Anyone who has ever opened his or her home to struggling strangers knows this: you're not just opening your home. You're binding yourself to those on the fringes of society in ways that continue long after the last plate is loaded in the dishwasher. You may be waving goodbye as the van of dinner guests from the local homeless shelter backs out of the driveway, but it doesn't end there. If you count these people as friends, not just guests, it never ends there.

✳ ✳ ✳

I first met Jill (not her real name) when she and several other homeless women from the downtown mission joined our church in Lansing, Michigan, for worship one Sunday morning. On the way to my suburban parsonage for lunch (my husband is a pastor now; we were appointed by the bishop to live here), Jill chattered with delight. Her Long Island accent rose in childlike excitement that changed to astonishment as we turned into my subdivision. "Oh, my Gawd," she gasped. "Oh. My. Gawd. Is this for real? But the houses all look the *same*! It's so creepy! It's like a horror movie!" By the time we pulled into my driveway, I was crying with laughter. Apparently, through certain lenses, the American dream can look like its own kind of nightmare.

We laughed during the meal. We passed the salt; we passed the tissues. If there's anything I've learned from those on the fringes, it's to shed pretense and social niceties as quickly as possible. And there was just no pretending with Jill. "I don't know that I believe in God today," she said to me, gaze direct but watery, "but I think I might believe you when you talk about Jesus." Well, then, let's talk about Jesus. Drop the formalities. What else is worth talking about, really?

My path crossed with Jill's on and off after that: occasionally she would come to church, or I'd run into her on the city bus, or she'd call asking for prayer in a simple, childlike, doubting kind of way. In time, she drifted out of orbit.

Then came the night one autumn that a colleague of mine and I were supposed to go out and celebrate our book contract. Both of us miraculously had arranged childcare. I had not only showered but was dressed up—because this mother of little kids was going somewhere *fancy*, dammit. Wiping baby slobber off my collar, I felt almost like a professional. But just as I picked up the keys and headed out the door, the house phone rang. It was Jill. She had moved into a new apartment. Her fiancé had just been arrested. She was hysterical. She wanted to die—in fact, she assured me repeatedly this would happen. Soon. Tonight.

I cradled the phone against my neck while frantically texting my husband on my mobile. *Call 9-1-1 now*—and included the address. And then I ran to the car.

It was a long half-hour winding through dark city streets, the beginning of flurries in the air. I was hoping for emergency lights to help me find the place, but her building was quiet. I buzzed her number, and there she was, wailing in the hallway at the sight of me. The police had come for a well check and determined she was fine.

Do you know the smell of poverty? Of hopelessness? It hangs on you for days. When we ask to bear someone else's burdens, that's not one we ask for. But there it was: I still smelled it days later, hidden in the folds of my coat, the coat that rested on her chair for three hours while we talked about God and Jesus and suicide and her fiancé's good heart and the fact that she could find no joy, no love, no *feeling* in the world.

"The only place I find peace," she said at one point, "is at church." "Of course," I said, "because Jesus is there." We agreed that Jesus was also here, in this barely lived-in apartment with the boxes and the mess and the emptiness. We prayed. She promised not to harm herself; we both would call her case manager in the morning. It was enough to go on, for now.

I was bound to Jill just as God has bound God's self to us by becoming human in Jesus. For life. Forever. I won't fix her. But I can sit with her in the mess.

✳ ✳ ✳

I watch him amble away, the boy in Union Station. That's my son, I realize. That's my first homeless guest, and Jill, and many subsequent others. I'm heartsick that what he needs in this moment is what I can't give him: a fix, to be fixed, to save this situation, his life. I'm not enough.

Jesus, I think.

Jesus.

Sunday, Day Thirty-Six

Neighbors

DEBORAH DICKERSON

I live in Vermont. It's the New England state that jockeys continually for first place as the least religious state in the country according to Pew Research. Christian friends from more churched parts of the country make glib comments about the perceived difficulties of my living in a godless place (as if such a place exists). And yet Vermont is the place where I have been most significantly shaped spiritually by its beauty, the community of small towns and churches, the slower pace of life, and even the spiritual spareness, the hunger.

I am currently in a Bible study feeding on the Gospel of Luke. I noticed that Jesus is completely comfortable around the seemingly least religious individuals, including Matthew's unsavory tax collector friends, a sinful woman, lepers, the demon-possessed, and the centurion from the enemy Roman army commended for his faith. Many of the religious elite—who should know better, should understand the signs pointing to Jesus' identity (and probably do)—are threatened by his presence, his claims on their lives, and his challenge to their power structures. They are the ones trying to trap him in his words and deeds. They are the ones trying to kill him. I wonder if Jesus dreaded those encounters with the religious. I wonder if he preferred the company of sinners— those who understood their own need. Religious Christians can be just as contentious as the religious leaders of Jesus' day. Sometimes, it's easier to be with non-religious neighbors who view us as an oddity in their lives. Their questions might be more curious than hostile in nature. They might even ask us on occasion to wing "some thoughts and prayers" on their behalf.

I imagine Jesus being completely comfortable in a barn with our local undocumented Mexican migrant workers milking cows at 4:00 a.m. on a cold January morning or singing with the Jamaicans on their special H-2A agricultural visas while they pick apples in orchards during early autumn when green drains from the leaves of trees. I imagine Jesus reading a picture book surrounded by toddlers and their weary parents for children's story hour at the local library. Or Jesus walking with a scout troop on the first Saturday of May as they join other Vermonters in the ritual of picking up trash for Green Up Day. I see Jesus sitting with students on the lawn of the local college (or even the pub) and encouraging them to seek the wisdom that comes from above. Or sitting beside the elderly with dementia, listening to their stories. Jesus would be telling stories, too, stories about the kingdom of God to feed their hunger. This is what we celebrate at Christmas. In Jesus, the kingdom of God broke into history; he came to seek those who are hungry for God's goodness in their lives.

One of my neighbors is Fran. She is ninety years old and comes to my church twice a week for an osteoporosis prevention class in our fellowship hall. She arrived in class after Christmas wearing a Chuck Norris sweatshirt from her grandchildren, who think she is "badass." I think she is too. About thirty percent of the class are women from my church; the rest come from the community. Over a dozen years, friendships have formed, and there are always plans among various members to play bridge, see a movie, or drive to Gail's house in March to see her lambs. I guide the warm-ups, the stretching, and the weightlifting, and Fran is the life of the party. She is the complainer-in-chief, the class clown, and our well-loved storyteller who keeps us laughing. Her stories about her neighbors' antics, the local wildlife, the latest scam artist who called her, her $1 bikini that was too good of a deal to pass up, and her adventures as a gemologist are so entertaining that we almost forget the hard work we are engaged in as we move through various muscle groups.

Fran recently needed eye surgery. The initial repair did not hold, so there was another painful surgery followed by bleeding that did not stop and put pressure behind the retina. My bold and funny friend had a crisis threatening her vision and her independent life. This was the first time I asked her for permission to put her situation on our church's prayer chain. "Yes, please. This repeat will be a bit dicey and if not successful, I'm in a bit of trouble. Thanks for the outside help. All is welcome." In that short text, she acknowledged that she was up against something that she did not have much control over. She acknowledged her fear and her need for help, even supernatural help. She received an outpouring of cards, offers for rides, and prayer support for peace and healing. I don't know if she will ever move from the exercise class in our fellowship hall into our sanctuary for worship, but I do know that she has been fed by the love of God's people. She said, "I am overwhelmed by all the kindness."

Most weeks I attend a poetry workshop. The other attendees range widely in their religious and political views. A significant percentage of the group is Jewish. Another significant percent is agnostic or atheist. This group seems to function like a church for many of the poets; it's the place where each member has a distinct voice. Their contributions are taken seriously no matter how new they are to writing. It's the place for sharing important ideas, joys and sorrows, celebrating publications, and receiving encouragement. It's a place to be fed and challenged to grow. In a poetry workshop, all the big topics are written about and discussed—love, faith, art, sex, and the passing of time, which of course leads to death.

David is our facilitator. He has identified some of my poems as prayers before I have. He has been a source of encouragement to me in my writing and my life. In his leadership, David models compassion for struggling writers, for those who grieve, for the mentally ill and the marginalized. He warns me when another participant has submitted a poem that is critical of the church, evangelicals or Jesus. He worries that I will be offended. I assure him that I appreciate the concern and that I am not easily offended. In fact, I often find the criticisms valid. David is also open about being a Jew who does not believe in God. He has mentioned several times that God appears in his poems from time to time. I think, *Yes, of course God shows up in your poems. You are a poet. Popping into the poems you write is one way he reveals himself to you,* though I have yet to say it aloud. I know he is attracted to goodness. And God is good. I expect God will continue to reveal himself to David—in beauty, in poems, and through relationships.

I met Danielle shortly after she had completed a brief sentence at the women's correctional facility for issues related to drunkenness and disorderly conduct after significant life trauma. Her goals were sobriety and regaining custody of her daughter. Our initial meetings took place in my car as I drove her to appointments. She was attending AA meetings and praying to a "higher power." She knew that she needed strength beyond herself to put her life back together, but I didn't have a sense that she felt connected to Jesus or the "higher power." A few months into our developing relationship, the Covid-19 pandemic began, and our communication was restricted to phone calls. About once a month, we called each other and shared our struggles. She talked about her limited contact with her daughter and all that was stacked against them for reunification. I shared my struggles in having a parent with Alzheimer's living in the house with me and my husband. When I offered to close our conversations with prayer, she always said, "Yes, please."

We have known each other for more than two years now. Danielle regularly calls me with updates about her life and to request prayer. She has remained committed to sobriety, counseling, and regaining custody of her daughter. She has employment and a place to live, which are both challenges after incarceration. She is taking classes to finish a college degree. Despite all the positive changes, the child custody battle continues, along with faulty assumptions and accusations lobbed against her. It wears her down. She has complex post-traumatic stress disorder (CPTSD) related to an assault.

After our last time of praying together, I asked her to consider going to church. I suggested that church might seem like just an additional activity in her life already full with classes, employment, counseling appointments, travel to see her daughter, and meetings with her probation officer. But she needs worship to feed a spiritual tank that is running on empty. She agreed that she needs connection with worship and a faith community.

She needs what Fran and David need, what I need—a connection with Jesus, "who, being in very nature God, did not consider equality with God something to be used to his own advantage; rather, he made himself nothing by taking the very nature of a servant, being made in human likeness" (Phil 2:6-7 NIV). He walked among the people of his day inviting them to follow him and be fed with the bread of heaven. We pray, "Give us this day our daily bread" to fill our hunger. And then we share it with our neighbors.

✳ Live Lovingly ✳

MARILYN McENTYRE

Anne Sexton once wrote of a child, "Love grew around her like crabgrass." It's one of my favorite of her many surprising lines, partly because it makes me smile and remember a particular child, and partly because it gets at something true about love: when it finds a place to take root, it spreads in all directions and finds new places to take root and cling. Love is rooting and branching everywhere—the life force that spins electrons and divides cells and gathers people in smiling, fascinated circles around small children.

A coach I worked with used the expression "in love" more broadly and precisely than most of us who associate it with a particularly besotted state of romantic attraction. When he spoke of a person who worked or played "in love," he seemed to suggest that that person inhabited a particular zone of consciousness or state of awareness, or that love was a kind of weather bubble—a warm place of particular clarity where ambient light gathered. I think of the way he taught me to imagine love when I read Paul's charge to the Ephesians, "Walk in love."

Love, as The Troggs' song "Love Is All Around" reminds us, is all around, and in our very bodies: "I feel it in my fingers, / I feel it in my toes." Love flows and circulates. We receive it and release it like the breath our lives depend on. From the heart of God it comes to us like light from distant stars, unimaginably swift, burning through cold and darkness.

We are meant and designed to be light-bearers and agents of love. We are invited to dwell in God's love and from that safe place, like a child looking out on the world from the safety of loving arms, to let our own circles of love ripple and widen with every encounter. We are truest to our own nature and most faithful to creation when we live lovingly.

But of course love has, as Virginia Woolf reminds us, a thousand shapes. A thousand faces. A thousand facets, each burning with its own brilliance. Like light, it splays and breaks into discrete colors, some of them dark. Love may be, as St. Paul writes, patient and kind, but it can also be edgy, articulate, able to speak truth to power, fierce with conviction, and strong and mysterious as the power of an aikido master.

To live lovingly is to wield a force like a light saber and also to inhabit a force field in which everything is charged with life. And it is to discern prayerfully where and how to call forth that force in the service of the defenseless and the vulnerable. Now more than ever those prayers prepare us for the responsibilities we must take on as bombs are exploded in city streets and lobbed into olive groves where unsuspecting children play.

The great feast of Christmas reminds us of how a vulnerable child came into the world to bear and embody God's own unfathomable love, arriving not in regal majesty, but needing human care, and subject to the imperfect, unpracticed human efforts: "Word within a word, unable to speak a word," as T. S. Eliot mysteriously put it. The same love that exploded into galaxies lay sleeping in the arms of a young mother whose consent to his coming represented all human turning toward the source of all love.

And so we celebrate. And so a thousand Madonnas are adorned and altars bedecked and homes "made fair" and gifts given and the poor more generously gathered and fed this time of year. And we, who wander like sheep into thickets of distraction and sloughs of greed, are brought back into love, reminded, reassured, and released once again like those same sheep who "safely graze," after all, beside streams of living water.

Nativity Figure Speaks

JEANNE MURRAY WALKER

I felt it, riding through the afternoon,
how nights are getting shorter and it's cold
and then the baby shifted in my womb
and the innkeeper sent us to his sandy field.

I did what I was made to do. And now
who knows what else is possible? God's breath
moves against the soft nose of the cow.
The moon shines on this shed and on the path
where you stand watching.
                                        Who are you?
I am the round yon virgin of your song.
You are the sky the light is passing through.
You're the iron moonlight, the sweet fresh-
smelling hay, the shepherds, the three kings.
Believe we live and free us from this crèche.

✳ # Midnight Migrations

AMANDA LEE DeVOS NEWELL

✳

✳

I open my window
　　to hear before I see
　　　　a flock of geese
　　　　　　fly V overhead
　　　　　and cut right through
　　　the soft O
of the moon.

The next night
　　I walk down to the lake
　　　　and listen to
　　the incoming splashes,
　　　the raucous
　　　　　honk, Honk, HONK:
　　　　　　the praise of a congregation
who has come so far
　　through the deep dark
　　　　to find itself once again
　　　　　in warm shallows.

　　　　　The true size of that body
　　　　　　remains invisible to me,
　　　　yet I feel the enormous joy
of communion.
　　　I feel the unified spirit
　　　　of hearts
　　　　　headed for the same destination.

Come Winter, at Night

AMANDA LEE DeVOS NEWELL

an owl cries
     through fir trees
her sad series of *whys, whens, hows*

that are given no answer,
     and then she wonders:
Who's there?

Then it's as if the whole forest
     begins to talk—
no longer just

one
     solitary
hoohoo,

but one
     answers another,
          and then another—

much like us,
     as we face despair
flightless, lightless,

we question
      the dark
alone

until we discover around us
      a congregation
of reminders:

I am here.
    We are here.
        He is here.

Wednesday, Day Thirty-Nine

✳

His Hands on Their Heads

✳

✳   ✳

About that time the disciples came to Jesus and asked, "Who is greatest in the Kingdom of Heaven?"

Jesus called a little child to him and put the child among them. Then he said, "I tell you the truth, unless you turn from your sins and become like little children, you will never get into the Kingdom of Heaven. So anyone who becomes as humble as this little child is the greatest in the Kingdom of Heaven.

"And anyone who welcomes a little child like this on my behalf is welcoming me" (Mt 18:1-5 NLT).

One day some parents brought their children to Jesus so he could lay his hands on them and pray for them. But the disciples scolded the parents for bothering him.

But Jesus said, "Let the children come to me. Don't stop them! For the Kingdom of Heaven belongs to those who are like these children." And he placed his hands on their heads and blessed them before he left. (Mt 19:13-15 NLT)

Let Them ✳

JILL PELÁEZ BAUMGAERTNER

✳

He names them: Samuel, Isaac, Mary,
all of the anonymous daughters of Jephthah,
the infant of Bathsheba,
and those forty-two children who laughed
at bald Elisha and were torn limb from limb.

Let them come.
Let them push their small shoulders
into the crowd of Rachel's children.
Let the Holy Innocents stand so close
they can see the beating pulse
of his temple.

Let them come.
All of those with tiny wrists,
small ankles, pudgy or thin arms,
round bellies from feast or famine.
Let them feel the breath of God
on their precarious necks.

Let the armless child from Iraq
rest on his knee. Let the Vietnamese
girl with burning skin remember
his cool fingers.

Let them come. Do not hinder them.
Smooth the path, clear the way
for him to feel the press of them,
the warmth of their perilous bodies
next to his.

Epiphany

LUCI SHAW

When a real epiphany comes for me, I recognize it as God dealing with me in a direct, irrefutable way. One such sighting came in the fall of 1988. I was teaching poetry at Regent College in Vancouver, Canada, while living an hour away, in Bellingham, Washington.

The Pacific Northwest is known for its rains that fall steadily for days (or weeks) and for clouds that hug the earth, shrouding the landscape in a gentle gloom. Just a few miles in from the coast rise the Cascade Mountains and, spectacular among them, Mount Baker.

I wrote in my journal:

For weeks I've driven my highway, north in the morning, then south again at the end of the day. The mountains are clearly marked on the map, but they might as well not exist, lost as they are in clouds, obscured by drizzle, fog, haze. Then, some morning, unexpectedly, a strong air from the sea will lick away the fog and allow the sun to shine cleanly. And Mt. Baker, towering magnificently beyond the foothills, unbelievably high above the other mountains, is seen for what it has been all along—immense, serene, unmovable, its dazzling, snow-draped profile cut clear against a sky of jewel blue.

Today it happened. The mountain "came out"! I kept turning my eyes from the highway to look once more at its splendor, wanting to be overwhelmed again and again. It is heart-stopping. I can't get enough of it. And I can never take it for granted. I may not see it again for weeks.

It's God, showing me a metaphor of himself. I mean—he's there, whether I see him or not. It's almost as if he's lying in wait to surprise me. And the wind is like the Spirit, sweeping away my foggy doubt, opening my eyes, revealing the reality of God. Annie Dillard's words say it for me: "It was less like seeing than being for the first time seen, knocked breathless by a powerful glance...."

The word *epiphany* means, literally, "a showing." Traditionally, this showing is accompanied by light; we need light in order to see what is being shown us. And light is something that every human heart longs for and responds to. Day holds all the clarity of brilliance and vision—a certainty—where night brings blindness in the unknowing dark.

Jesus himself was personified as the Sun of Righteousness. Even in our diurnal rhythms, day/night/day, sunset is a figure of chill, aging, and death, while the appearance of the morning sun over the horizon's blackness speaks of warm hope and a new beginning. This response is so universal that when God explains himself to us in Scripture as light—the "true Light that lightens everyone"—we recognize the glory and joy of the image.

In liturgical churches, the Feast of Epiphany is the first feast in the calendar new year. Traditionally it falls on January 6 and celebrates the "showing" of the infant Christ to the Eastern sages in Bethlehem, where they had been led, curiously enough, by a star—a small, glowing, celestial flashlight for their dark path from the orient. The star of Bethlehem is to me a remote spark from the universal light toward whom the wise men were traveling, a coal from the blaze that sprang up when God struck his match in the world.

This event—the manifestation of Jesus to the wise men—is the sighting of God in the flesh, an event the church has seized upon that lights up the first week of our dark, wintry new year. But it is not the only one. Often, at the most unexpected moments, Scripture—and life—bring into our focus other sets of sightings, or epiphanies. Perhaps every miracle that Jesus did, every healing, every teaching, was a new showing of himself.

Jesus said, "Blessed are the pure in heart, for they shall see God." This means that as humans are purged and rinsed clean, as they grow more transparent so that their souls are like windows, they are invited into deeper seeings of God, appearings that have often been terrible—that is, full of terror. Think of Moses on Sinai, of Daniel in Babylon, or of John on Patmos confronted with the blazing glory of the One like the Son of Man. Think of the series of fearsome sightings in the early chapters of the Gospel of Luke, when the admonition "Don't be afraid" was an assurance badly needed by each of those confronted with a heavenly visitation— Zechariah, Mary, the shepherds.

Though the sudden, dazzling presence of God has often seemed a fearful thing for the humans involved, it has always been what I most dearly long for. God has sometimes disclosed himself to me in ways that I can only call indirect, through metaphors from life and nature and the Bible, through moments with a sense of significance about them, when everything suddenly danced into place. The inexplicable exhilaration of those rare instants redeemed, for a time, my days of chaos and confusion.

It's not difficult to remember or experience, with our baptized intellects or imaginations, times of new understanding *about* the almighty. The Bible is full of metaphors that reveal God in images such as a rock, a banner, a mother hen, a lover, an artist. But all too often I have felt "in the dark" about God himself—unable to see *him*. Even though Jesus came close to us in the incarnation, it all seems so long ago. I long for the immediate, unmistakable knowledge of his presence now, the smell, the sight, the touch of him. Even though its heat and light might scorch me, such "hard evidence" wouldn't be too hard for me to take.

I have often felt like the three disciples climbing down from Mount Tabor after the transfiguration, unable to see ahead through the mist that covered the mountain after Jesus appeared to them. Sometimes, in the days following my husband's death, when life was very dark indeed, other people would come to me with stories of their dreams or visions of Harold, which seemed to them like epiphanies. Paula D'Arcy "saw" him among the worshipers on her church balcony on All Saints' Day, "beaming with light and joy," as she expressed it to me in a phone call.

My friend Georgia Bosch dreamed that she and her husband were dining at our house, and after helping me in the kitchen she reentered the dining room to see Harold sitting at the head of the table. "Luci thinks she's all alone," he told her, "but I'm watching, and I know everything she does." Margaret Smith has often *heard* God's plans and purposes for me in prayer. These were comforting assurances, but at a remove, circuitous, second-hand, not direct enough to satisfy me. Why didn't the Lord give *me* a vision? Why couldn't I, in the mountaintop sun with Peter, James, and John, see Jesus with his face shining "like the sun, and his clothes dazzling white as light"?

Both by nature and definition, epiphanies of the divine are rare. Exceptional. That is the way we recognize them for what they are. Like miracles, they are not part of the normal fabric of our lives. And they are nearly always individual rather than corporate experiences, personal rather than public spectacles. We cannot participate in the angel's announcement of the incarnation to Mary except in imagination. Paul, going to Damascus, fell to the ground when the flash of light from heaven surrounded him. But those traveling with him saw nothing. And when someone today tells us of their supernatural revelation from God, we cannot enter into it except by a faint, cognitive stirring.

I wonder if you will feel that stirring as I tell you about a Tuesday morning that same fall at Regent College when God made himself known to me even more unmistakably. Dr. James Houston came into my office, sat down, and said, almost without preamble, "I know that often in your life you have felt abandoned by a father who was away preaching most of the time, by uncaring friends, now by Harold, whose death has left you alone, and by God. I believe that you will only find an answer to your sense of abandonment in *self-abandonment*, in willingness to give away to God yourself, your identity. You've been walking through a long, black tunnel. Soon you will see light ahead of you, and when you come out of the tunnel, you'll find yourself on the edge of a cliff. *You must throw yourself off the cliff edge and trust that God will catch you in his arms.*" Startling words. They made me shiver because I had indeed felt the chill of that abandonment. But they also brought me the tingle of anticipation. I knew I needed to take this wise friend's words seriously. I needed to think through all the implications of his message from God to me, with its prophetic ring, so that I would know *how* to throw myself off the cliff.

The word Jim had used, *abandon*, appealed to me. All my life I'd been urged by spiritual leaders to "yield," to "surrender" to God, to "relinquish" my idols. Through overuse those words had lost their impact and freshness for me, but the wildness, the impulsiveness of the word *abandon* challenged me to take this new risk.

On Tuesdays, people at Regent meet in small groups to pray and grow together in friendship. Journal in hand, I went to my car with Laurie, a young mother, her baby, and the baby's stroller, which I had to load into the trunk. We drove to the home where our group met, and when I got there I realized, with a sick jolt of panic, that the journal was gone.

Frantic, I rushed back to the campus in the car and checked in my office, then followed my cold trail through the building and out again to the parking lot. No journal. As I walked back to my car in the rain, I felt the interior tremor, the recognition of what this event really meant. My journal is an extension of me, as important as arm or leg. In it I feel my life condensed, myself embodied: my most personal observations and ideas and reflections are expressed and recorded in it in a way intensely valuable to me as a tracking of my life. I could buy another new, blank journal and start in again to reflect on its pages, but to lose this one, three-quarters full, was like losing myself. *Losing my self* . . . Suddenly I knew what was happening—God was pressing in for my gift. He was telling me the *how* of abandonment.

I gulped, then found myself saying, inwardly, *This is almost too painful to contemplate, but yes, if my journal stands for what you want from me, I'll give it up to you. I'll abandon it, and throw myself off the cliff edge. But oh, please be there to catch me!*

Still shaking, I drove back to the prayer group. As I pushed open the front door, Laurie met me and said, beaming, "Karen Cooper just phoned to say she'd found your journal in a puddle in the middle of University Avenue. You can pick it up at her house this afternoon." I realized that as I drove away from Regent, it must have fallen off the top of the car, where I'd put it while stowing the stroller in the trunk.

Later, when Karen, my student and friend, handed the soggy journal back to me, there was a tire print stippled across its familiar, ugly orange front cover; its back cover was half ripped off; and the coiled binding of its spine was bent and flattened. But it had been given back to me. I had made the jump. God had made the catch.

Karen and I prayed our exhilaration and thanks. She wondered aloud to me: "And some people doubt the personal involvement of God in their lives? Why should I, who knew you so well, and knew where to call you, be the one to stop my car in the rain, to find out what it was that had caught my eye, lying in that puddle? Why did I stop at all? Traffic was heavy. There were scores of cars and bicycles and pedestrians traveling on that busy street. But I found the journal and saw your name was written on the front."

In the same journal that night I wrote the story, and its conclusion:

> If I am willing to abandon my will to God, broken like the spine of this journal, imprinted with God's own tire-track signature, he will give it back, and my identity with it. Oh, I feel it so profoundly, pierced to the core with its reality. God does care for me. He has not abandoned me. I have been "knocked breathless by his powerful glance." He showed himself, beaming his light to my heart in a true epiphany.

Friday, Day Forty-One

Christmas: The View from Prison

JEANNE MURRAY WALKER

Bing Crosby croons "I'll be home for Christmas" as I pull into a muddy space in the parking lot. I snap the radio off and run with my head down through the spitting sleet, my sneakers splashing toward the door of a large, squat, mint-colored building. The front door is bolted, so I press the red button and shiver in the pelting ice until a buzzer goes off: a guard has briefly unlocked the door. Hearing the zzzzz, I lunge. But even my split-second dive doesn't catch the door before it automatically locks again—as if the door itself were eager to keep the prisoners inside and everyone else out.

The waiting room, when I finally get in, gives no hint of Christmas. It's beige, cheaply tiled, with dirty blond wooden chairs arranged in a small square. A heavy-set, uniformed female guard appraises me, then growls, "Get that pocketbook outta here."

"Yes, ma'am."

"Just your keys, your books, and a pencil."

I thank her and step back into the freezing drizzle.

Months ago, I signed up to teach writing to the women at Baylor Women's Correctional Institution. I had never known a prisoner, nor ever stepped inside a prison. I promised to show up on a Friday afternoon in October for a meeting with the volunteer coordinator and one of my university faculty colleagues, who, I discovered, had also committed to teaching at Baylor.

The training session was run by a short, bald, uniformed officer, who warned us not to reveal our names to the "offenders," as he called the women. We were not to invite them to talk about their personal lives, and we were not to reveal anything about ourselves, even our names, unless we wanted to find them stalking us years later, after they had been released. "These women are expert cons," he said. "If they weren't when they got to prison, they've learned by now."

At that, a woman in a lovely blue silk scarf raised her hand. "What do you mean—cons?" she asked.

"They'll use you."

"Use us for what?" she asked politely.

"To bring bullet in," he said. "Drugs. That's what they call drugs. Or to try to get them a jackrabbit parole." And he went on to explain that we'd be easy for them to dupe, inexperienced as we were. "For example," he said, "don't wear that kind of scarf around your neck in here. I shouldn't have to explain why." Everyone chuckled grimly.

He went on. No jewelry. (I slid my wedding rings onto the candle on our dinner table Friday mornings before I drove to Baylor.) No jeans, bright colors, or sleeveless shirts, no short skirts or tight pants, no coded clothing of any kind, not even red and green at Christmas. We were forbidden to bring the women presents or to offer them cookies or candy. Surprisingly, we were permitted to call them by their first names, though the staff called them by their last names, as in "Nelson, what are you doing over there?" I thought about that with irony later: that Jody was called by the name of the man she had married and—after years of abuse—had finally killed.

When I returned to the waiting room after sequestering my purse in the trunk of my car, my colleague Deb had arrived. When Deb and I were called to enter the cell area, two massive sides of an enormous iron door slid apart. An hour later, fifteen women in loose-fitting maroon prison smocks and pants filed into the prison's cement-block room to sit in front of us at cheap blond wooden desks. Some gazed at us coolly, some smiled, some stared defiantly, and one slapped rhythm on the table with her hands, only to be hooted at and reprimanded by others sitting around her. Several intimate groups of two sat close and murmured to each other. The guard who had escorted Deb and me to the room left us sitting together at the front desk with the chattering women under the glaring florescent lights.

My colleague and I persuaded the women to get quiet, finally, then namelessly introduced ourselves. We handed them the composition books and pens and colorful folders I had bought for them. They eagerly jockeyed and scrambled to get their favorite colors. Then we handed out a syllabus for the first few weeks' lessons. They listened as each of us spent a couple of minutes explaining our vision for the class. We would assign photocopies of reading they could do during the week. We would talk and write about it together the following week.

They didn't raise their hands; they shouted, sometimes over one another. We suggested that they talk one at a time, which would require that they raise their hands. They booed and murmured disapproval. I worried that they must think we were turning out to be like all the other teachers they'd ever had, rule-driven and condescending. I felt disappointed; I had hoped that some of the women, at least, would be eager learners, happy finally to find a way to develop their skills. I think a few were, but many had failed at reading and writing so regularly in the past that they couldn't summon another good try.

At the second class, fewer women showed up. We handed out copies of short essays, explaining that to get into college or to apply for a job they would probably have to write short answers to employers' questions. To learn to write well, we argued, it would be helpful to read examples of good writing and use them as patterns.

As the months went on, my colleague and I pieced together the facts, that the women in our class lived in three or four different prison units and they were "in" for assorted offences—drug and alcohol crimes, shoplifting, embezzlement, assault, disorderly conduct, and, of course, murder. We knew that serving time in prison, no matter how short, might destroy their chance of being hired for a good job in the future. The record of their consistent attendance in a writing class might help them to prove their worthiness for future jobs. In fact, steady attendance in the writing class could help those who had not yet been sentenced to document their good behavior to a judge, who might shorten their sentences.

But only four or five of the women showed up for class consistently. The following week even these women dribbled in twenty minutes late, telling us they had been released late by guards from their different units. Only three or four said they had done some of the reading, and maybe they had, but no matter how we tried, we couldn't convince them to talk about it. As we encouraged them to participate, the women drummed their pencils on the table, they fussed with their hair. They made jokes about one another and flared into petty quarrels.

When I read their first three-paragraph essays, I was struck by how many of them muddled verbs. Verbs, of course, document actions that happen in the past or in the present or in the future. "Doing time" in prison apparently had messed with their ability to conceptualize time—not only on paper, but in their own lives.

I wondered: if they can't tell themselves the stories of their own past, how can they understand themselves? How can they change?

In spite of severe warnings during our volunteer orientation at Baylor not to engage in personal conversation, after almost four years, I know a little about who the ladies are. One is resigned to being treated by prison doctors for what she says is a brain tumor. She expects to die in her cell. Several claim they are about to be released. Most of them spend their days watching TV, and the shows are what they talk about the most. They laugh more easily than I do. Some of them seem motherly and have found another more vulnerable prisoner to take under their wings. A few are smart-alecs; several are sober and motivated students. Most of them are lovable.

Together, over years, they have formed a complex social and political status and relational system, which I have only begun to figure out. They are not allowed to own much: soap, a toothbrush, some snapshots. One of the women owns a thesaurus, and when the others don't know what a word means, they pester her till she looks it up. One, whose daughter goes to junior college, asked me to bring the novels and poems her child was reading so she could read them at the same time; she reeled off titles and authors of obscure nineteenth-century British novels. I brought her the paperbacks she wanted from my own shelves.

It's Christmas now again, and I know that our women will not celebrate what for me is among the most holy days of the year. They will not be gathering to sing "Joy to the World." They will not be setting a table with Lenox or any other kind of china. They will not be roasting a turkey and mashing potatoes for their kids. They will not be opening presents; they will most certainly not be giving any. Visitation rules limit each of them to two adults and one child or one adult and two children per day, and they can have

visitors for only one hour around noon. There is increasing literature that argues prisons may help purge criminals from society,
but the American way of imprisonment leaves these women worse
when they are discharged from prison than when they entered.
They leave prison bereft of their families and work; they often
revert to their old neighborhoods and their crime buddies.

Meanwhile, at Christmas the choir at St. Peter's here in Philadelphia this week will be singing "O Little Town of Bethlehem"
and "Hark the Herald Angels Sing" and "Joy to the World." The
music will thrust us into time-out-of-time, to celebrate the birth
of the holy child into human history. As Frederick Buechner has
written, "history itself falls in two at the star" that stood above
the Christ child in the manger. Our celebration of Christmas
with its soaring music, its winsome clothes, its Christmas cards,
its beautifully decorated trees, its feasts, its family gatherings, its
vibrant creativity offers us every year a heavenly rest from what
can sometimes seem, even to those of us outside prison, a daily
slog. The church calls non-holy days "ordinary time." Once a year
Christmas interrupts ordinary time, elevating us to a different
sense of time—transcendence—as we celebrate God's coming to
us from beyond time.

But the strict, rule-governed drudgery of prison makes transcendence seem impossible for its inmates. The prison building
itself offers little to the women except routinized ugliness. If
beauty can save the earth, as Greg Wolfe argues, what chance do
these women have? Finally, the most horrible punishment the
women at Baylor endure is to never be able to leave ordinary time.
Prison makes many of them grimly aware that they will be putting
in one dull, repetitive day after another, many of them for decades.
I imagine they will spend the coming Christmas Day in their cells,
as usual. They tell me they have been forgotten by their people.

Heading toward my fourth Christmas at Baylor, I know none of our women have written long enough or clearly enough for me to help them find a place to publish their work. Maybe they will never write their stories. Instead, I have written this for them.

I have a lot in common with these women. We love our children. We are all "doing time" until we die, though I have been blessed with liberty and choices they can only dream of now. Ironically, getting to know inmates in the Women's Correctional Institution has made the world a less frightening place for me than it might be if all I did was to drive by the prison and think of the women as dangerous others. My truest Christmas gift this year has been my discovery that words can sometimes connect me with the women at Baylor in love instead of fear.

Saturday, Day Forty-Two

When I Look at the Night Sky

PSALM 8 NLT

O Lord, our Lord, your majestic name fills the earth!
  Your glory is higher than the heavens.
You have taught children and infants
    to tell of your strength,
silencing your enemies
    and all who oppose you.
When I look at the night sky and see the work of
      your fingers—
    the moon and the stars you set in place—
what are mere mortals that you should think about them,
    human beings that you should care for them?
Yet you made them only a little lower than God
    and crowned them with glory and honor.
You gave them charge of everything you made,
    putting all things under their authority—
the flocks and the herds
    and all the wild animals,
the birds in the sky, the fish in the sea,
    and everything that swims the ocean currents.
O Lord, our Lord, your majestic name fills the earth!

A Sky Full of God's Children

MADELEINE L'ENGLE

I walk out onto the deck of my cottage, looking up at the great river of the Milky Way flowing across the sky. A sliver of a moon hangs in the southwest, with the evening star gently in the curve.

Evening. Evening of this day. Evening of my own life.

I look at the stars and wonder. *How old is the universe?* All kinds of estimates have been made and, as far as we can tell, not one is accurate. All we know is that once upon a time or, rather, once before time, Christ called everything into being in a great breath of creativity—waters, land, green growing things, birds and beasts, and finally human creatures. This was the beginning, the genesis, not in ordinary Earth days; the Bible makes it quite clear that God's time is different from our time. A thousand years for us is no more than the blink of an eye to God. But in God's good time the universe came into being, opening up from a tiny flower of nothingness to great clouds of hydrogen gas to swirling galaxies. In God's good time came solar systems, planets, and ultimately this planet on which I stand on this autumn evening as the Earth makes its graceful dance around the sun. It takes one Earth day, one Earth night, to make a full turn, part of the intricate pattern of the universe. And God called it good, very good.

A sky full of God's children! Each galaxy, each star, each living creature, every particle and subatomic particle of creation—we are all children of the Maker. From a subatomic particle with a life span of a few seconds to a galaxy with a life span of billions of years, to us human creatures somewhere in the middle in size and age, we are made in God's image, male and female, and we are, as Christ promised us, God's children by adoption and grace.

Children of God, made in God's image. How? Genesis gives no explanations, but we do know instinctively that it is not a physical image. God's explanation is to send Jesus, the incarnate One, God enfleshed. Don't try to explain the incarnation to me! It is further from being explainable than the furthest star in the furthest galaxy. It is love, God's limitless love enfleshing that love into the form of a human being, Jesus, the Christ, fully human and fully divine.

Was there a moment, known only to God, when all the stars held their breath, when the galaxies paused in their dance for a fraction of a second, and the Word, who had called it all into being, went with all his love into the womb of a young girl? Did the universe start to breathe again, the ancient harmonies resume their song, and the angels clap their hands for joy?

Power. Greater power than we can imagine, abandoned, as the Word knew the powerlessness of the unborn child, still unformed, taking up almost no space in the great ocean of amniotic fluid, unseeing, unhearing, unknowing. Slowly growing, as any human embryo grows, arms and legs and a head, eyes, mouth, nose, slowly swimming into life until the ocean in the womb is no longer large enough, and it is time for birth.

Christ, the second person of the Trinity, the Maker of the universe or perhaps many universes, willingly and lovingly leaving all that power and coming to this poor, sin-filled planet to live with us for a few years to show us what we ought to be and could be. Christ came to us as Jesus of Nazareth, wholly human and wholly divine, to show us what it means to be made in God's image.

Jesus, as Paul reminds us, was the firstborn of many brethren.

I stand on the deck of my cottage, looking at the sky full of God's children, and know that I am one of them.

Acknowledgments

The editors would like to thank the members of the Chrysostom Society for their good fellowship and pleasant encouragements as we pursued this project together. And also our spouses, Duncan and Sharon, for their bouts of patience, support, and forbearance. Al Hsu and the entire team at InterVarsity Press have been more than helpful as the book has taken shape, and we also want to express our appreciation to the Dallas Willard Research Center of the Martin Institute at Westmont College for a generous grant in support of this anthology. Finally, our thanks and praise to the One who came, in the flesh, to give us reason to celebrate. May our small words participate in the Word who is before all things and in whom all things consist.

Contributors

Sarah Arthur is the author of more than a dozen books for teens and adults, including *A Light So Lovely: The Spiritual Legacy of Madeleine L'Engle* and *Once a Queen*, the first in a young-adult fantasy series. A graduate of Wheaton College and Duke University Divinity School, Sarah has served as preliminary fiction judge for the *Christianity Today* Book Awards and is a founding codirector of the L'Engle Writing Retreats.

Jill Peláez Baumgaertner is the author of six collections of poetry, including the recently published *From Shade to Shine: New Poems*. She has also edited a collection of poetry, written a textbook/anthology, and published *Flannery O'Connor: A Proper Scaring*. She has served as the poetry editor of *The Cresset* and *First Things* and currently serves as poetry editor of *The Christian Century*. She has edited an anthology of poetry from *The Christian Century* that will be published in 2023. Past president of the Conference on Christianity and Literature, she is professor emerita of English and former dean of humanities and theological studies at Wheaton College. She has written song texts and libretti for many composers, most recently for Michael Gandolfi, whose Cantata, based on Psalm 139, was performed by the Boston Symphony Chamber Orchestra. She and her husband live in Chicago.

St. John Chrysostom (ca. 349–407) was one of the preeminent Greek fathers of the church—a preacher of such eloquence that he was given the nickname *Chrysostomos*, or "Golden-Tongued." Born in Antioch, he eventually became Archbishop of Constantinople, where he played a reforming role. In both cities he preached against the veneration of statues of the Roman emperor and his family, a stance that led to his banishment and death. In his lifetime he composed over three hundred biblical homilies—and over two hundred of his letters remain extant. To this day his "Divine Liturgy" serves as the basis of worship in Eastern Orthodox and Eastern Catholic Churches of the Byzantine Rite. As an exemplar of eloquence and integrity, John Chrysostom is a worthy patron saint for our society.

Deborah Dickerson works as a guardian *ad litem* (child advocate) for the Vermont Judiciary. She is a contributing editor for *Voices*, an online art magazine for Memorial Baptist Church. She is also a member of the Otter Creek Poets in Middlebury, Vermont. Her poems have appeared in *Voices, Zig Zag Lit Mag*, and *Tiny Seed Journal*, and have been exhibited at The Birds of Vermont Museum. She is married to Matthew Dickerson, her partner in the canoe, on the ski trails, and in life. They spend time regularly with their sons, daughters-in-law, and grandson, who (amazingly) all live in Vermont.

Matthew Dickerson is the author of several published books, including works of fiction, creative nonfiction, spiritual theology, apologetics, biography, and literary criticism. His novels include both fantasy literature (*The Gifted, The Betrayed,* and *Illengond*) and medieval historical fiction (*The Rood and the Torc*). His narrative nonfiction titles include most recently *The Voices of Rivers* and *A Fine-Spotted Trout on Corral Creek*. His works of spiritual theology and apologetics include *Disciple-Making in a Culture of Power, Comfort, and Fear* and *The Mind and the Machine: What It Means to Be Human and Why It Matters*. He is best known, however, for his writings about C. S. Lewis and J. R. R. Tolkien, including *A Hobbit Journey, Narnia and the Fields of Arbol,* and *Ents, Elves, and Eriador*. Matthew lives in Vermont with his wife, Deborah, and teaches at Middlebury College.

Leslie Leyland Fields is the award-winning author of twelve books, including *Forgiving Our Fathers and Mothers, Surviving the Island of Grace,* and *Your Story Matters: Finding, Writing and Living the Truth of Your Life*. Her books are translated into nine languages. She served for five years on the editorial board of *Christianity Today* and taught at University of Alaska and in Seattle Pacific University's MFA program. She does audio narration as well for her.BIBLE, Oasis Audio, and Our American Stories. Every summer she hosts the Harvester Island Writers' Workshop on her family's fish camp island in Alaska with guest writers such as Philip Yancey, Ann Voskamp, and Bret Lott. In the winters, she speaks at conferences, churches, and retreats around the world on matters of faith, writing, and culture. She also teaches Your Story Matters classes online to thousands and leads writing workshops training others to bring Your Story Matters workshops into prisons, classrooms, churches, homeless shelters, recovery groups, and anywhere people need to know they are seen, loved, and heard. You can find her online at www.LeslieLeylandFields.com.

Richard Foster is founder of the Chrysostom Society and Renovaré, an effort working for the renewal of the church in all her multifaceted expressions. He is the author of several books, including *Streams of Living Water*, *Prayer*, *Freedom of Simplicity*, *Sanctuary of the Soul*, and *Celebration of Discipline*, which has sold over two million copies worldwide. He and his wife, Carolynn, make their home near Denver, Colorado.

Diane Glancy is professor emerita at Macalester College. Recent books of poetry and prose include *Island of the Innocent: A Consideration of the Book of Job*; *A Line of Driftwood: The Ada Blackjack Story*; *Jigsaw*; and *Home Is the Road: Wandering the Land, Shaping the Spirit*. She is also the coeditor of the anthology *Unpapered*. Among her awards are two National Endowment for the Arts Fellowships, an American Book Award, a Minnesota Book Award, an Oklahoma Book Award, a Pablo Neruda Prize for Poetry, an Expressive Arts Grant from the National Museum of the American Indian, and a Lifetime Achievement Award from the Native Writers' Circle of the Americas. Native Voices at the Autry has produced four of her plays. Glancy's other books and awards are on her website, www.DianeGlancy.com.

Paula Huston, a National Endowment of the Arts Fellow, is the author of two novels and eight works of spiritual nonfiction. Her short stories and essays have appeared in numerous magazines, including *U.S. Catholic, The Christian Century, Books and Culture, America*, and *Story*, along with being anthologized in collections like *Best Spiritual Writing*. She taught writing and literature at Cal Poly, San Luis Obispo, for over ten years, was a faculty member in the California State University Consortium MFA in Creative Writing, and served as a mentor in creative nonfiction for the MFA program at Seattle Pacific University. A wife, mother, and grandmother, she is an oblate (lay member) of New Camaldoli Hermitage in Big Sur, California. Her most recent book, a history of this monastic community, is based on notes kept for over sixty years by an early American novice. *The Hermits of Big Sur* tells the story of what unfolds within this small and idealistic group of monks when medievalism must finally come to terms with modernism.

An emeritus professor of English at Houghton University, **John Leax** lives in retirement with his wife in the Genesee Valley of western New York. His books of poetry include *The Task of Adam, Tabloid News, Recluse Freedom*, and *Remembering Jesus*. His prose works include two collections of essays, *Grace*

Is Where I Live and *Out Walking*. He is currently working on a sequence of haiku-like poems responding to the journals of Thomas Merton and wasting his time sauntering in the words of Thoreau.

One of the charter members of the Chrysostom Society, **Madeleine L'Engle** (1918–2007) was an American writer best known for her young-adult fiction, particularly the Newbery Medal–winning *A Wrinkle in Time* and its sequels: *A Wind in the Door*, National Book Award–winning *A Swiftly Tilting Planet*, *Many Waters*, and *An Acceptable Time*. Among L'Engle's numerous books are autobiographical works and reflections on biblical stories: *Two-Part Invention*, *A Circle of Quiet*, *A Stone for a Pillow*, and *Sold into Egypt*. Her works reflect both her Christian faith and her strong interest in modern science.

Marilyn McEntyre, longtime professor of American literature and medical humanities, teaches, speaks, leads retreats, and writes about connections between language, spirituality, healing, and care of the earth. Her recent books include the second edition of *Caring for Words in a Culture of Lies*, *Speaking Peace in a Climate of Conflict*, *Where the Eye Alights*, *Dear Doctor*, and *The Mindful Grandparent*. Recurrent writing workshops include Approaches to Spiritual Autobiography, Writing from Inside Out, and Words and the Natural World. She teaches courses for Westmont College in San Francisco, and for New College Berkeley. She is also on the faculty of the "Sacred Art of Writing" DMin program at the Eugene H. Peterson Center, Western Theological Seminary, and of the "Forest Dwelling" program in aging and spirituality at the Oblate School of Theology, San Antonio. She takes particular pleasure these days in coaching working writers. More information is available at www.MarilynMcEntyre.com.

Benjamin Myers was the 2015–2016 Poet Laureate of the state of Oklahoma and is the author of four books of poetry: *The Family Book of Martyrs*, *Black Sunday*, *Lapse Americana*, and *Elegy for Trains*. His poems may be read in *The Yale Review*, *Image*, *Rattle*, *32 Poems*, *The Cimarron Review*, and many other literary journals. Myers lives with his wife and three children in Chandler, Oklahoma, and is the Crouch-Mathis Professor of Literature at Oklahoma Baptist University, where he directs the great books honors program. His essays have appeared in print and online for *First Things*, *The American Conservative*, *Oklahoma Today*, and other venues. His first book of nonfiction, *A Poetics of Orthodoxy*, was recently published by Cascade Books.

Amanda Lee DeVos Newell is a production editor at Lexham Press. She was born and raised in Steamboat Springs, Colorado, where when she wasn't playing outdoors, she was writing stories on an old typewriter. She received a BA in English from Westmont College, which ignited her interest in poetry and publishing. She has worked in a variety of writing, editing, and project management roles. She serves as the secretary-treasurer of the Chrysostom Society and lives in Bellingham, Washington, with her husband, Mathias. In her free time, you may find her reading, skiing, hiking, or making new recipes.

Gina Ochsner teaches writing and literature at Corban University and is on the faculty with Seattle Pacific's Low Residency MFA program. She is the author of the short story collection *The Necessary Grace to Fall*, which was selected for the Flannery O'Connor Award, and the collection *People I Wanted to Be*. Both collections received the Oregon Book Award. Her novels include *The Russian Dreambook of Color and Flight* and *The Hidden Letters of Velta B*. Ochsner is at work on another collection of magic realism/fantasy/speculative stories titled *A Shadow Curled Around Your Heart*. To find out more about Gina, please visit www.GinaOchsner.com.

Eugene H. Peterson (1932–2018) was a beloved Presbyterian pastor in New York and Maryland before returning to his native Montana to focus on his writing. In the last decades of his life, he also served as a professor of spiritual theology at Regent College in Vancouver, British Columbia. He is best known for his skillful paraphrase of the Bible known as *The Message*. Among his many other books written with pastoral sensitivity are *Working the Angles* and *A Long Obedience in the Same Direction*. His sensitivity, however, did not extend to contemporary popular music. Invited by his admirer Bono to attend a U2 concert, he reportedly sat through the entire event in pleasurable confusion.

Tania Runyan is an NEA fellow and the author of several award-winning poetry collections. Her guides *How to Read a Poem*, *How to Write a Poem*, and *How to Write a Form Poem* are used in classrooms across the country. Her poems have appeared in many publications, including *Poetry*, *Image*, *Harvard Divinity Bulletin*, *The Christian Century*, *Saint Katherine Review*, and the Paraclete book *Light upon Light: A Literary Guide to Prayer for Advent, Christmas, and Epiphany*. She and her family live in northern Illinois, where she teaches middle school language arts. Visit her at www.TaniaRunyan.com.

Before retiring, **James Calvin Schaap** taught literature and writing at Dordt University, Sioux Center, Iowa, for thirty-seven years. He has published many short stories and several novels, as well as *Startling Joy*, a book of Christmas stories. His nonfiction titles include *Things We Couldn't Say*, the wartime biography of the Dutch Resistance fighter Diet Eman. Most recently, he has published *Looking for Dawn* (a novel), *Up the Hill: Folk Tales from the Grave* (stories), *Reading Mother Teresa* (meditations), and *Small Wonders: A Museum of Missouri River Stories*. He contributes weekly vignettes from regional history on KWIT, an NPR station in Sioux City. He and his wife, Barbara, live just outside of Alton, Iowa, an open field away from the historic Floyd River.

Luci Shaw is writer-in-residence at Regent College, Vancouver. Author of over forty books of poetry and creative nonfiction, her writing has appeared in numerous literary and religious journals. In 2013 she received the annual Denise Levertov Award for Creative Writing from Seattle Pacific University. Recent work includes a poetry collection, *Angels Everywhere*, and a book for children, *The O in Hope*.

Robert Siegel (1939–2012) was the author of nine books of poetry and fiction. His poetry collections include *A Pentecost of Finches: New and Selected Poems*, *The Waters Under the Earth*, *The Beasts and the Elders*, and *In a Pig's Eye*. He received prizes and awards from *Poetry*, *Prairie Schooner*, *The Transatlantic Review*, the Ingram Merrill Foundation, and the National Endowment for the Arts, among others. His poems appeared in numerous journals and anthologies, including *Poetry*, *Prairie Schooner*, and *The Atlantic Monthly*. He also wrote several novels, including *Alpha Centauri* and the *Whalesong* trilogy, which received the Golden Archer and Matson awards. Siegel taught at Dartmouth, Princeton, and Goethe University in Frankfurt, and for twenty-three years at the University of Wisconsin-Milwaukee, where he directed the graduate creative writing program.

Daniel Taylor (PhD, Emory University) is the author of more than a dozen books, including *The Myth of Certainty*, *Letters to My Children*, *Tell Me A Story: The Life-Shaping Power of Our Stories*, *Creating a Spiritual Legacy*, and *The Skeptical Believer: Telling Stories to Your Inner Atheist*. He has also published a series of metaphysical mystery novels beginning with *Death Comes for the Deconstructionist*. He was a stylist for the *New Living Translation* of the Bible.

During its brilliant lifespan, he was a contributing editor for *Books and Culture*. Taylor speaks frequently on such topics as the role of doubt in the life of faith, the shape of a good life, and living as a reflective believer in a pluralistic world. He also conducts workshops on writing about your life as a spiritual legacy. In addition, he leads adult tours to various places around the world. His website is www.WordTaylor.com.

Dain Trafton was for many years a professor of literature and an occasional administrator in various colleges and universities in the United States and abroad. He has published scholarly books and articles on English, American, French, Italian and neo-Latin writers, including translations from Italian into English, personal essays, reviews, criticism, fiction, and poetry. Now retired from teaching and administrative work, he lives and works in northern New England, his native ground. He has been honored by election to numerous scholarly and literary societies, including Phi Beta Kappa. For a more detailed account, please visit Dain's webpage at www.DainTrafton.com.

Jeanne Murray Walker, who was born in a small Minnesota village, has written nine volumes of award-winning poetry, the latest being *Pilgrim, You Find the Path by Walking*. Named an Atlantic Monthly Fellow at Bread Loaf School of English when she was nineteen years old, Jeanne has been awarded many fellowships and prizes, among them a Pew Fellowship, a National Endowment for the Arts Fellowship, and eight Pennsylvania Council on the Arts Fellowships. Her memoir, *The Geography of Memory*, tells how she and her sister cared for their mother during a long decade of Alzheimer's. Jeanne served for many years on the editorial boards of *Image* and *Shenandoah* magazines. With Darryl Tippens, she edited *Shadow and Light: Literature and the Life of Faith*, an anthology of literature. She served as a Poetry Mentor in the Seattle Pacific University MFA Program and she taught at the University of Delaware for forty years, where she headed the creative writing concentration and organized some of the nation's first study-abroad programs. Jeanne and her husband are the parents of two and the grandparents of five. They live outside Philadelphia.

Walter Wangerin Jr. (1944–2021) was a Lutheran pastor and a professor of literature and theology at Valparaiso University in Indiana. He authored more than thirty books in his lifetime and was best known for his fables *The Book of the Dun Cow*, which won the National Book Award, and its sequel,

The Book of Sorrows. His work is honored in a recent collection of essays by members of the Chrysostom Society, *Songs from the Silent Passage*.

Paul J. Willis, now retired, served for many years as professor of English at Westmont College in Santa Barbara, California, where he lives with his wife, Sharon, near the old mission. He has published seven collections of poetry, the most recent of which is *Somewhere to Follow*. He is also the author of an eco-fantasy novel, *The Alpine Tales*; the young-adult novel *All in a Garden Green*; and the essay collections *Bright Shoots of Everlastingness* and *To Build a Trail*. He has served as poet laureate for the city of Santa Barbara and as artist-in-residence in North Cascades National Park. Each January he hosts a community reading of the poems of William Stafford on the banks of the Santa Ynez River in Los Padres National Forest. For more about Paul and his work, visit www.PaulJWillis.com.

Lauren F. Winner is an Episcopal priest and a professor of Christian spirituality at Duke Divinity School. She is the author of many books, including *Girl Meets God, Wearing God,* and *Still*. She lives in Durham, North Carolina.

Growing up in a strict, fundamentalist church in the South, **Philip Yancey** tended to view God as "a scowling Supercop, searching for anyone who might be having a good time—in order to squash them." As an adult, writing became Yancey's way of coming to terms with this past. He has authored over twenty-five books, each the result of candidly exploring painful or perplexing questions. In the process he has wrestled with God, with the church, and with fellow believers. Philip's books have garnered thirteen Gold Medallion Awards. He currently has more than seventeen million books in print and is published in over forty languages worldwide. In his recent memoir *Where the Light Fell*, Yancey recalls his lifelong journey from the toxic faith of his past to a life dedicated to his search for grace and meaning. It serves as a type of prequel to all his other books.

For more information about the Chrysostom Society, visit

WWW.CHRYSOSTOMSOCIETY.ORG

Permissions

Madeleine L'Engle, "Redeeming All Brokenness," in Madeleine L'Engle and Luci Shaw, *WinterSong, Christmas Readings* (Vancouver, British Columbia: Regent College Publishing, 1996). Used with permission of Charlotte Jones Voiklis.

Robert Siegel, "Annunciation," in *The Waters Under the Earth* (Moscow, ID: Canon Press, 2005). Used with permission.

John Leax, "Letter to Friends, Advent, 1990," excerpt from *Once Upon a Christmas: A Treasury of Memories*, ed. Emilie Griffin (Norwalk, CT: C. R. Gibson Co., 1990). Used with permission of John Leax.

Tania Runyan, "Angel at the Nativity," in Tania Runyan, *Simple Weight* (Lexington, KY: FutureCycle Press, 2010). Used with permission of Tania Runyan.

Tania Runyan, "Joseph at the Nativity," in Tania Runyan, *Simple Weight* (Lexington, KY: FutureCycle Press, 2010). Used with permission of Tania Runyan.

Philip Yancey, "In a Mad Mad World, God Welcomes Our Merrymaking," *Christianity Today*, December 21, 2021, www.christianitytoday.com /ct/2021/december-web-only/philp-yancey-christmas-mad-world-god -welcomes-merrymaking.html. Used with permission of Philip Yancey.

Paul Willis, "Christmas Child," in *Say This Prayer into the Past* (Eugene, OR: Cascade Books, 2013). Used with permission of Paul J. Willis.

Madeleine L'Engle, "O *Simplicitas*," in *Cry Like a Bell* by Madeleine L'Engle, copyright @ 1987 by Crosswicks. Used by permission of Shaw Books, an imprint of WaterBrook Multnomah Publishers, a division of Penguin Random House LLC. All rights reserved. Also used with permission of Charlotte Jones Voiklis.

Lauren F. Winner, "Jesus' Bloody Birth," Copyright @ 2015 by the *Christian Century*. Reprinted by permission from the December 20, 2015, issue of the *Christian Century*. www.christiancentury.org.

Jeanne Murray Walker, "Silent Night." Used with permission of Jeanne Murray Walker.

Tania Runyan, "Mary at the Nativity." Used with permission of Tania Runyan.

Tania Runyan, "Shepherd at the Nativity," in Tania Runyan, *Simple Weight* (Lexington, KY: FutureCycle Press, 2010). Used with permission of Tania Runyan.

James Calvin Schaap, "Winter Solstice." Used with permission of James Calvin Schaap.

Paula Huston, "Spreading Light in Our Wake," excerpt from "At the Source," in *Take Heart: Catholic Writers on Hope in Our Time*, ed. Ben Birnbaum (New York: The Crossroad Publishing Co., 2007). Used with permission of Paula Huston.

Paul Willis, "*Amo, Amas, Amat*," the third section of "Spokane: A Triptych" by Paul J. Willis. Copyright © 2005 by Paul J. Willis. Published in *Bright Shoots of Everlastingness: Essays on Faith and the American Wild* (WordFarm, 2005). Used with permission from WordFarm (www.wordfarm.net).

Luci Shaw, "A Blessing for the New Baby," in *Accompanied by Angels* © 2006. Wm. B. Eerdmans Publishing Company, Grand Rapids, MI. Reprinted by permission of the publisher; all rights reserved.

Madeleine L'Engle, "Into the Darkest Hour," in Madeleine L'Engle and Luci Shaw, *WinterSong, Christmas Readings* (Vancouver, British Columbia: Regent College Publishing, 1996). Used with permission of Charlotte Jones Voiklis.

Leslie Leyland Fields, "Let the Stable Still Astonish." Used with permission of Leslie Leyland Fields.

Leslie Leyland Fields, "No Silent Night." Used with permission of Leslie Leyland Fields.

Eugene H. Peterson, "Star" in *Holy Luck*, first edition © 2013. Wm. B. Eerdmans Publishing Company, Grand Rapids, MI. Reprinted by permission of the publisher; all rights reserved.

Luci Shaw, "Star Song." Used with permission of Luci Shaw.

Marilyn McEntyre, "Live Lightly," *Adverbs for Advent* (Eugene, OR: Wipf and Stock, 2017). Used with permission of Wipf and Stock Publishers, www.wipfandstock.com.

Paul Willis, "Freeman Creek Grove," in *Visiting Home* (San Antonio, TX: Pecan Grove Press, 2008). Used with permission of Paul Willis.

Walter Wangerin Jr., "Maundy Thursday." Used with permission of Ruthanne Wangerin.

Madeline L'Engle, "Tree at Christmas," in Madeleine L'Engle and Luci Shaw, *WinterSong, Christmas Readings* (Vancouver, British Columbia: Regent College Publishing, 1996). Used with permission of Charlotte Jones Voiklis.

John Leax, "Vigil: Christmas Eve, 1991," excerpt from *Once Upon a Christmas: A Treasury of Memories*, ed. Emilie Griffin (Norwalk, CT: C. R. Gibson Co., 1991). Used with permission of John Leax.

Dain Trafton, "In a Museum: To My Granddaughters," *Stonework*, Issue 5 (2007). Used with permission of Dain Trafton.

Leslie Leyland Fields, "The Miracle of Sir Nick." Used with permission of Leslie Leyland Fields.

Philip Yancey, "Melancholy Angels," Philip Yancey Blog, December 22, 2018, https://philipyancey.com/melancholy-angels. Used with permission of Philip Yancey.

Luci Shaw, "The Golden Ratio and the Coriolis Force." Used with permission of Luci Shaw.

Paul Willis, "The Forest Primeval," in *Visiting Home* (San Antonio, TX: Pecan Grove Press, 2008). Used with permission of Paul Willis.

Paul Willis, "Piano." Used with permission of Paul J. Willis.

Gina Ochsner, "Shine," *St. Katherine Review*, vol. 1.2. Used with permission of Gina Ochsner.

Paul Willis, "How Are You, My Friend?" by Paul J. Willis. Copyright © 2018 by Paul J. Willis. Published in *To Build a Trail: Essays on Curiosity, Love & Wonder* (WordFarm, 2018). Used with permission from WordFarm (www.wordfarm.net).

Lauren F. Winner, "Christmas and the Cross: Luke 2:22-40," Copyright © 2008 by the *Christian Century*. Reprinted by permission from the December 16, 2008, issue of the *Christian Century*. www.christiancentury.org.

Sarah Arthur, "The Least of Us," Awst Press online post, September 18, 2017, https://wendy-walker-tlod.squarespace.com/essay-series/the-least-of-us. Used with permission.

Marilyn McEntyre, "Live Lovingly," *Adverbs for Advent* (Eugene, OR: Wipf and Stock, 2017). Used by permission of Wipf and Stock Publishers, www.wipfandstock.com.

Jeanne Murray Walker, "Nativity Figure Speaks." Copyright © 2007 by the Christian Century. Reprinted by permission from the December 11, 2007, issue of the Christian Century, www.christiancentury.org.

Jill Baumgaertner, "Let Them." Used with permission of Jill Baumgaertner.

Luci Shaw, "Epiphany" in Madeleine L'Engle and Luci Shaw, *WinterSong, Christmas Readings* (Vancouver, British Columbia: Regent College Publishing, 1996). Used with permission of Charlotte Jones Voiklis and Luci Shaw.

Madeleine L'Engle, "A Sky Full of Children," excerpt(s) from *Bright Evening Star: Mystery of the Incarnation* by Madeleine L'Engle, copyright © 1997 by Crosswicks, Ltd. Used by permission of WaterBrook Multnomah, an imprint of Random House, a division of Penguin Random House LLC. All rights reserved. Also used with permission of Charlotte Jones Voiklos.